A
MINDFUL
LIFE

To Dureene & Bob

Best Wishes for
A Good life

Vivek ...

11/9/06

A
MINDFUL
LIFE

**A Brain Surgeon's Personal
Experiences and Philosophical
Reflections on Living Life Fully**

Vivekanand
Palavali, M.D.

Blue Sun
Press

A MINDFUL LIFE
Copyright © 2006 Vivekanand Palavali, M.D.
Published by Blue Sun Press

Though this is a true story, and the events told in this story are entirely my own, to respect confidentiality, all the names have been changed.

For more information about this title, please contact:

www.surgeonscut.com
vilasune@aol.com

Book design by:

Arbor Books
www.arborbooks.com

Printed in the United States

A MINDFUL LIFE
Vivekanand Palavali, M.D.

1. Title 2. Author 3. Self-Help / Motivational / Inspirational / Success

Library of Congress Control Number: 2006900081
ISBN: 0-9777311-0-3

To my parents and my beautiful wife, whose love and sacrifice are unforgettable, and to my two boys, who give me immense joy.

Acknowledgements

I would like to acknowledge all the patients and their families whose pain, sadness and joy I will always carry, to some extent, as part of me.

I thank and appreciate the patience of my wife and boys, who did not receive my full attention these past few months as I was engrossed in the writing of this book.

Introduction

"Don't take life for granted." That simple but profound saying is so common that its truth sounds almost trite. But not many people actually live accordingly. That is, until some abrupt, unexpected and devastating tragedy strikes them or their loved ones, resulting in either loss of life or limb. Suddenly their lives take a dramatic and desperate course. Then, sadly, many realize that they have been going about their daily routines oblivious to life's simple pleasures and, in general, to life itself. It will be too late when they realize that life and wellness were taken for granted all along.

Do you ever wonder why people live this way in spite of being aware of life's fragility and fleetingness? It may be

1

because they do not contemplate the act of living fully enough. They may also think that personal tragedies are random and will not happen to them. The reality is, unfortunately, contrary to such belief. Then, how can one make people stop for a moment, examine their way of life and alter their perspective so that the "cup of life" will be filled to the brim and relished till the last drop, daily? This book is an attempt to do just that.

As a brain surgeon, I come across situations frequently in which patients of all ages either perish or become paralyzed from accidents, ruptured brain aneurysms, brain tumors, gunshots and strokes. Those unfortunate people and their families are shocked that such tragedies happened to them. Dealing with these highly emotional life-ending or life-altering situations has made me realize and remember two very important truths. First, that life is very fragile and, second, that nobody is immune to such devastation. Those truths have influenced my philosophy of life profoundly. I savor each day like a single line in a poem of unimaginable beauty.

The heart-breaking ordeals of some patients, as they held on to life, taught me invaluable life lessons. Many people do not face life-and-death situations every day and may therefore need to open their eyes a little wider to see what they already know—that each day should mean everything to us. My experiences as a brain surgeon have taught me that nobody can predict when this beautiful and exciting "bubble of life" may burst. I hope that sharing some experiences that led to this recognition will make readers contemplate and alter their perspectives on daily life, allowing them to enjoy every moment deeply and deliberately. I know it's easy to forget in the course of the everyday that each second is essential; but, in the ER, seconds are sometimes all you have.

The attitude of taking life for granted is not just an American, but a universal, one. For that reason I feel this book will interest anyone who does not want to, some time in the future, regret not having lived life to its fullest potential. It will also appeal to those eager to relish life everyday and that includes, I believe, almost every human being.

"Tomorrow's life is too late. Live today."

—Martial

Tomorrow May Not Come

Unlike my usual mornings, this was not a good one. To be honest, it started as a morning of mourning, when I walked into one of the brain trauma intensive care rooms. The patient was lying in bed, still and lifeless. His face was puffy and eyes were closed shut. There were many different tubes coming out of various parts of his body: a breathing tube from his mouth connected to a ventilator; a tube from his stomach coming out of his nose; others from his brain, bladder, neck and wrist. His name was Brad.

Brad's parents and sister were at his bedside with the sadness of the last night etched on their faces. Their eyes were red as if they did not sleep. They were probably weeping for some time, too, especially after hearing the test results. In fact I could see tears rolling down his mother's cheeks. It was very quiet in the room, the silence broken only by the rhythmic hiss of the ventilator, which was, essentially, breathing for Brad. Even that hiss was going to be silenced soon. It would be futile to leave the machine on. Early that morning, Brad had an Electroencephalogram (EEG) done to see if there was any brain activity at all. There was none.

The events of the previous few days, leading to that terminal moment, flashed through my mind.

My encounter with Brad began when my beeper went off, a few nights ago. It was around 11 p.m. and I just got into bed after a long day of surgeries. I was looking forward to enjoying the simple pleasure of finally being able to lie down and stretch my body, after standing for some hours in the operating room. I picked up the beeper from the bedside table and looked at the number. It was the emergency room (ER).

"Oh, no." It was difficult to suppress a tinge of disappointment as I reached for the phone. After a few rings, a courteous female voice was on the other side.

"ER. Can I help you?"

"Dr. Palavali here. I was paged."

"Hold on, Doctor. Let me find out who paged you." I

could hear her screaming, away from the phone, over the commotion in the background, "Dr. Palavali is on line!"

"Hi, doc, this is David," the trauma surgeon said, picking up the phone a minute later. "We have a boy coming in, estimated time of arrival 15 minutes. I wanted to give you advance notice before he gets here. Sounds like he has severe head trauma."

"What happened?" I asked.

"He was a passenger in a car that was hit head on by a drunk driver going 60 miles an hour. He has a big scalp laceration and possibly a fractured skull. His Glasgow coma scale (GCS) is 4."

GCS measures the level of consciousness. A '4' qualifies as a severe head injury and meant that the boy was in a coma.

"How are his pupils?" The most important information I, as a brain surgeon, needed. If one pupil was dilated big and did not become smaller when light was flashed into that eye, it usually denoted a life-threatening emergency, requiring immediate intervention. It's a tense situation neurosurgeons do not look forward to.

"I was told that they were equal and reacting to light," David said. I relaxed a little.

"Was there any hypoxia?" I asked. Possibly compounding the problem, he might have had inadequate oxygen (hypoxia) or blood supply to his brain if he either had additional injuries to his lungs or heart or he lost a lot of blood.

"Yeah, the paramedics found him gasping for air, I don't know for how long exactly. They said it took a long time to extricate him. He was pinned under the dashboard. It sounds like a bad one," David replied.

"I'll be right there." I hung up and got out of bed. My wife, lying next to me, closed the book she was reading and asked, "Do you have to go back to the hospital?"

I nodded my head and said, "ER."

"I am sorry," she said sympathetically. She knew I could use some sleep, but accidents don't happen at our convenience.

I got dressed as fast as I could and got into my car. While driving to the hospital, images of the accident popped into my mind. Flashing lights of police cars, white ambulance, shattered pieces of glass scattered on the road, a smashed and twisted car, paramedics struggling to release the trapped, unconscious boy, who was breathing in agony, and blood everywhere, its bright color a contrast to the stark scene.

The boy was in a race against time. Even though his pupils were equal, he could develop a large blood clot any time, in or around the brain, pushing his brain to the opposite side and putting his life in jeopardy. This could be happening even as I was on my way to the ER. The pressure on the brain must be relieved as quickly as possible by surgical evacuation of the blood clot, through an opening cut in the skull. Every minute was crucial.

I did not feel tired anymore; instead, because of the potential life and death situation, I was alert and could feel my heart beat a little faster. My lack of sleep was insignificant compared to this boy's ordeal.

I parked my car in the lot right in front of the ER and half-ran into the trauma room. There were quite a few doctors, residents, nurses and physician assistants (PA), attending to Brad. The scene was noisy and appeared chaotic, like any initial resuscitation of a level 1 trauma patient would. But there was a method to this madness, supervised by the trauma leader.

One of the nurses was starting a large bore line into a vein, in case he needed blood transfusion, while another was placing a catheter into the bladder so his urine output could be measured and checked for blood, suggesting injury to the kidneys. The respiratory therapist was adjusting the settings of the breathing machine. One of the PAs was checking his extremities to see if any bones were broken. Everybody was talking over each other and moving around hurriedly, creating apparent pandemonium. David and the ER physician were reviewing the chest x-ray to make sure the breathing tube was in the proper place and that there were no findings suggestive of injury to the lungs or heart. They saw me and started towards me.

This is how I first saw Brad, lying on a stretcher, stripped of his clothes, with a breathing tube through his mouth connected to a ventilator. His body was absolutely motionless except for the rhythmic rise and fall of his chest, synchronized with the hiss of the breathing machine. His head was wrapped in a roll of gauze that was soaked through with blood. A few drops of blood were dripping down his face, which was swollen and bruised black and blue. His eyes were closed.

As I was putting on a pair of gloves to examine him, I called his name. He did not open his eyes. I rubbed on his sternum but the eyes did not open, even to that deep stimulation; but his arms stiffened and rotated inwards. That kind of movement, called decerebrate rigidity, meant he had very low brain function and indicated a poor prognosis. I opened his bruised and swollen eyelids and turned the flashlight on. The pupils were still equal and constricted sluggishly. Overall, the examination revealed that there was only minimal activity of a deeper part of the brain, called the brainstem. He was, indeed, deeply comatose.

I unwrapped the bandage and saw a big cut on the left side

of his forehead extending up to the top of his head. On close inspection I could see a fracture of his skull. Soft, yellowish brain tissue was seeping through the fracture, an ominous finding suggesting there was severe pressure in his brain. I put a new piece of gauze on the wound and told one of the nurses to put some pressure on, hoping to slow down or stop the bleeding.

I asked, while pulling off the bloody gloves and staring at an unrecognizable face, "How old is this boy?"

"Seventeen," David replied, standing next to me. I shook my head in pity, an instantaneous emotional reaction. It was probably hard for my subconscious to accept such devastation occurring to a teenage boy, bringing the full and exciting life ahead of him to an abrupt end.

"Let's get a CAT scan of the head," I told David.

Within the next few minutes, Brad was moved onto the CAT scanner, adjacent to the trauma room, and I was looking at the images of his brain and skull forming on the monitor. The scan showed the skull fracture on the left side of his fore-head with a few fragments of bone dug into the underlying brain. There was no large blood clot; instead, the whole brain was severely swollen.

"What do you think?" David asked.

"Well, there is no clot to evacuate, but I need to elevate the depressed fracture and debride (clean) the wound." I paused for a moment and then continued, "He is not going to do well."

"OR is on standby; I'll tell them the patient is on the way," David said as he reached for the phone.

"Thank you," I said. "Is his family here?"

"Yes. They are waiting in a room. The social worker is with them."

"I'll go talk to them."

I was leaving the ER through the trauma room to find Brad's family and saw, in a pile on a counter, the ripped and bloody tuxedo that Brad wore. I stopped abruptly and one of the nurses, noticing my reaction, said, "He was on the way home after the prom." It took some time before I could come out of that initial shock and make myself walk again. The timing of this tragedy could not have been more chilling.

"I'll take you to the family, Doctor," the social worker said, waiting outside the trauma room.

We started walking silently. I had my head bent down, contemplating Brad's neurological condition, which was so bad that I did not think there was much that could be done to save his life. His chances of any meaningful functional recovery, enough to lead an independent life, were even worse and almost zero.

"Very sad, isn't it, Doctor?" My thoughts were interrupted by the social worker's sympathetic words.

We entered the room where Brad's mother, father and sister were sitting anxiously on a sofa. Every second of waiting must have been excruciating to them. His mother was visibly shaken and the expression of fear on her face was obvious. Her lips were trembling. His father was trying to compose himself but I noticed a film of tears in his eyes. His sister was crying silently, tears rolling down her face. They already had some idea that Brad's condition was very serious.

"This is Dr. Palavali, the neurosurgeon," the social worker

introduced me. I leaned forward and softly held each one's hand, briefly and silently. The situation was too grim to say any niceties. I pulled a chair a little closer and sat across from them.

"I am very sorry to meet you all under these circumstances." I paused for a moment that felt like eternity.

"I don't have any good news for you." Another pause.

"Brad has very bad injuries to his head. He is in a deep coma."

His mother gasped and put her hands on her chest.

"There is a big fracture on the left side of his head. There is no blood clot inside or around the brain that needs to be taken out, but..." I got interrupted by his dad's hopeful question.

"That's good, isn't it, Doctor?"

I shook my head from side to side.

"Unfortunately, it's not like that. Even though there is no big blood clot, the brain is very swollen. His brain got jarred severely and there is a lot of pressure in it. In fact," I hesitated for a moment, debating if I really needed to mention this, "I could see brain tissue seeping through the fracture."

"Oh, God," his mother almost screamed and his sister covered her mouth with her hands to muffle her cry.

His father closed his eyes. The pain in their faces was heart-wrenching.

After a brief and awkward silence, I continued. "There is a big cut in his scalp and a few pieces of bone are digging into the brain. I need to clean the cut, remove the fragments of bone and close the scalp as soon as possible. Otherwise his brain may get infected. I don't think the surgery is going to affect his prognosis much. Most of the damage is already done."

Pause.

"He is in critical condition right now."

As much as I hate being in the horrible situation of having to tell the family that their loved one might die, it would be irresponsible not to give as realistic a prognosis as possible, even though I knew that was not what they wanted to hear. It would be wrong to give them any false hopes.

"No matter what I do there is a possibility that he may not survive this. He may stay in a coma for a long time or forever or he may improve somewhat. I am not sure at this point if he will improve enough to have any meaningful function. The first three days are crucial. If he wakes up and moves his arms or legs, then there may be some hope; otherwise it will be a very poor prognosis."

His mother shook her head as if she did not want to believe any of what I was saying. His sister wiped the tears off her cheeks but they streamed down again instantly. His father slowly lifted his head and asked, "When are you going to do the surgery?"

"Right away. It will probably take two hours. I am also going to place a brain pressure monitoring device on the right side," my hand automatically went to the right side of my head to illustrate where it would be. "The monitor is going to measure the pressure in his brain continuously and help me treat any increased pressure. There is a small possibility of more bleeding or infection from the surgery itself."

His father nodded his head in understanding.

"I will come and talk to you as soon as surgery is done," I said.

"I'll take you to the surgery waiting room," the social worker, sitting behind me all along, said to the family.

"We want you to do everything you can, Doctor," his father said softly.

"He is going to make it," his mother said, while rocking her body back and forth. "He has always been a fighter."

As I rose up from the chair his mother could not control the tears any more and buried her face in her hands. I gently touched her shoulder, shook his father's hand and turned to leave the room. I could hear his mother's sobs in the hallway.

I was walking alongside Brad's bed, which was being wheeled to the operating room, feeling very sorry for Brad and his family. It was difficult not to let their sorrow and emotional turmoil affect me. During our brief interaction, I watched them go through the whole range of emotions: disbelief, denial, shock, sadness, doubt if Brad would pull through, hope that he might and, finally, fear of possibly losing him. Unfortunately, in Brad's situation, as hopeful as his family tried to be, I was very doubtful of his survival, knowing what I knew as a brain surgeon. I looked at Brad's face and his eyes were still shut. He might never open them again, but I was determined to give him the best possible chance.

In the operating room, after Brad was anesthetized, I shaved his hair, matted with blood. The cut and fracture were more extensive than they initially appeared. I went to scrub my hands as one of the nurses cleaned the wound.

I put on a sterile gown and gloves and placed sterile drapes around the wound. I separated the edges of the wound and removed hair that had gotten driven into his brain at the time of impact. I drilled the edges of his broken skull and removed the pieces of bone that were digging into his brain. There was some bleeding from lacerated arteries and veins, which I stopped by cauterizing them. The covering membrane of the brain, called dura, was torn! Bruised, bluish-red brain could be seen through the tear.

I was careful not to extend the tear any more than I absolutely had to, looking for any blood clots under the dura. With so much pressure in his brain, if I enlarged the opening further, it would mushroom out through the opening and cause more damage. It would be impossible to get the extruding brain back in. I washed the wound with a copious amount of saline solution to flush out any bacteria and sutured the tear. I closed the scalp cut and placed a brain pressure monitor on the right side of his head, behind the hairline. The pressure in his brain, intracranial pressure (ICP), was elevated much more than normal. Not a good sign.

I left the operating room and changed out of my scrubs by my locker, knowing what I would have to do next. I went to Brad's family in the waiting room and explained what had been done. I told them, "The pressure in his brain is high, as predicted. It may increase in the next few hours or days. We will try to control it but it may be impossible. It can increase so much that it may lead to brain death."

His mother covered her ears; she did not want to hear those terrifying words. But I had to give them some idea of what to expect in the near future.

Over the next few days, despite every possible intervention, I could not prevent the pressure from escalating to dangerous levels. The pressure inside the skull was elevated so much that it prevented his brain from getting adequate blood supply and oxygen. I talked to Brad's family, daily, about his progressively worsening prognosis. As days passed by I saw their initial optimism and denial gradually replaced by an understanding of the inevitability of his death.

Eventually Brad's brain activity became less and less and reached a point where none could be detected. There was no more hope.

I distinctly remember the night when I had to tell them that depressing news. I felt the lump in my throat. "I am sorry to say that when I examined Brad just now, I didn't see any evidence of brain activity."

Everyone was silent. The mood was one of finality and acceptance, or it could have been emotional exhaustion that drained them of any expression.

Nothing could fill the void of Brad's loss. I kept shifting my gaze among them to avoid any prolonged eye contact, which, I thought, would be hard to bear.

"What do we do now, Doctor?" his father asked.

"I will order an EEG to see if there is any brain activity at all. It will be done first thing in the morning. If it confirms that there is none, which I suspect will be the case, I will have to declare him brain dead. Then we will have to withdraw ventilator support."

His mother's face had a blank expression, reflecting the emptiness in her heart.

"Even after the ventilator is turned off, his heart may beat for a few minutes before stopping."

Nobody spoke for a while. I told them that I would see them after the EEG was done and left the room.

It was around 1 a.m. as I was driving home. The roads out

of town were dark and empty, similar to my state of mind. Just as, in life, one can experience only one moment at a time, all I could see was the part of the road immediately in front of me, illuminated by headlights. Like the future, which could not be foreseen, I could not see the road beyond. Like moments of life passing by, the lane markings on the road were zipping by.

The EEG recording early that morning showed just a flat line, confirming that there was no brain function. Brad was declared brain dead.

I came back to the present moment.

It was difficult to keep my sadness from expressing itself. "I am very sorry about Brad." The words took forever to come out of my mouth.

His mother nodded, "We appreciate all you have done, Doctor. Thank you very much." She walked towards me and gave me a gentle hug. His father extended his hand and said, "Thank you."

I shook his hand firmly as if to convey that I understood their grief. My heart was sorrowful and, for a moment, I could feel my eyes tear up. I couldn't help, at that moment, feeling their sadness deep in my heart even though, as a brain surgeon, it was not unusual to come across so many similar situations. Was Brad's death especially moving because he was too young to die? Was it because, as I was told, he was a very good boy with a bright future ahead of him? To accept any life coming to a sudden and unexpected end is hard; a promising young life like Brad's makes it even harder.

I could not stay in that room any longer and headed for the door. As I was about to leave, I had to look, for one last time, at all the get well cards and pictures of Brad, with his family and his dog, that were taped to the wall across from him. My eyes stopped for a second on a picture of Brad, handsome in a tuxedo, with his beautiful date next to him. Both of them had wide smiles on their faces, full of life. I turned my head and looked at Brad's face, swollen, still and lifeless. What a terrible contrast! At that moment, the reality that life was very fragile hit me like lightning. All it took was a fraction of a second for the accident to happen, putting an end to a lively, young and promising life.

After I left the room, the ventilator was withdrawn. Brad's family wanted to be next to him when his heart beat for the last time. Within ten minutes, the heart rate became slower and weaker. At 11:15 a.m., the line on the EKG became flat, as his mother, father and sister were holding his hands. Brad was pronounced dead. There was no more tomorrow for him.

* * *

"We have only this moment, sparkling like a star in our hand… And melting like a snowflake. Let us use it before it is too late."

—Marie Beynon

> "Past is a dream,
> Future is a fantasy,
> Today is the reality."
>
> —Buddha

Buddha Principle

On the evening of Brad's death, I was sitting alone in my backyard. I could not get his death off my mind. My mood was like the overcast sky above. Thoughts and questions regarding the preciousness of every moment and the possibility of an unpredictable, instantaneous end stormed my consciousness, making me restless. Those thoughts were not strange to me. In the past there were occasions of intensely emotional, dramatic life and death situations, inherent to my profession, which made me wrestle with such questions. But on that day, after witnessing Brad's short life cease, it felt like a tornado of philosophical introspection about how I should live, love and enjoy every moment had touched down in my mind with full force. The thought of how life could end in an instant kept coming back. It could have been me involved in that accident. No one could predict exactly what unfortunate mishap would happen and when. In my work, I come across enough patients of different ages whose deaths or debilitation came upon them suddenly and prematurely from various causes, ranging from ruptured brain aneurysms, severe strokes and brain hemorrhages to fatal falls, gun shots and car accidents. Catastrophic possibilities were any and many.

I looked at the pond reflecting the gray clouds. Unlike the still water, my mind was racing. To think that tragedies strike only strangers, not us, would be mere wishful thinking. There were personal instances when family members, friends and colleagues expired, shockingly abruptly. One of my cousins was on an excursion with her classmates, slipped on a wet rock in a stream, hit her head on the rock and died even before she could be taken to the hospital. She was 20 years old, about to graduate from engineering school. I will never forget the misery on her parents' faces for a long time after. A close friend of mine went to San Diego with his wife and two sons on vacation. While on the beach, he literally dropped dead from a massive heart attack. To visualize his sons crying over him was heart-breaking. He was 39 years old and never had any indication that there would be a fatal problem with his heart. He was an internist, too. A colleague of mine, an orthopedic surgeon, was watching a movie in a theater in his hometown, where he went to visit his family. His breathing failed suddenly due to a blood clot in his lungs. I distinctly remember him telling me, just a few days earlier, that he planned on working hard for another three years and then retiring, so that he could enjoy life. He was 45 years old. His death taught me that there was always a possibility that our well-intentioned plans might not be realized. Another doctor who I knew very well was called about an emergency situation in the hospital, on a snowy, wintry night. On her way there, her car skidded on the icy road and hit a utility pole. She died on the spot. Her husband went into chronic depression. To realize that these untimely tragedies were not all that uncommon was quite unsettling.

I wondered if Brad or his family ever anticipated that anything like this could have happened to them. What kind of dreams and future plans did he have? Were there many wishes, some of which could have been fulfilled but were put off, experiences that could have been enjoyed but were postponed, for whatever reason, to a tomorrow that never came? Brad was young enough that he might not have thought seriously, in the context of life's fragility, about his wishes, dreams and future. For millions of people of all ages, including me, going through the daily grind without any attention to the possibility of sudden catastrophe was as normal as waking up every morning. The natural tendency of humans was to take life for granted.

I had always been somewhat puzzled about why we mostly lived for the future, oblivious of today. We did not enjoy life's little pleasures as much as we could, even though it cost us practically nothing. Usually all it requires is a change of perspective to get the most out of everyday life. My perception was that most people woke up every morning to "exist" rather than "live." Many would be the people who, despite their awareness of the fleeting nature of life, waited until after an incredible, personal tragedy to realize and regret that living had been postponed all along. Unfortunately, only then is the idea of living life fully everyday given its due attention and examination. Sure, nobody prefers to dwell on unpleasant thoughts of potential tragedy. But only by giving such thoughts necessary contemplation at some time in our lives (better sooner than later), can we grasp the simple yet profoundly significant fact that life is very precious and incredibly fragile. That understanding could enlighten us enough to appreciate, exquisitely, the value, beauty and joy of life, as it passes by, like a river, never to come back. We would not want to regret the things we wanted to do but never did, the places we wanted to go but never did and the feelings we wanted to express to our loved ones but never did because tragedy struck at an inconvenient time. It would be too late for any of those wishes to be realized after we were incapacitated or dead.

Since the beginning of my neurosurgery residency, dealing with patients going through unimaginable suffering humbled me. It impressed upon me that as beautiful and exciting as life is, it could be extinguished at anytime. That impression influenced my attitude to respect life and created a healthy sense of urgency to enjoy life, but Brad's death, additionally, drove the point home. Fortunately I did not have to experience any truly personal tragedy; instead, I learned from the unfortunate lives of some of my patients. Just as certain lives ended abruptly, it was possible that any day could be my last. I did recognize that it seemed pessimistic to let such a depressing thought be the driving force behind my daily living, but if it reminded me to savor each sweet, fleeting moment, such thought then becomes inspirational and motivational.

I vowed to myself that I was going to get the best out of every moment, to the most possible extent. I was not going to just "exist" but "live" every day. I would not say that we should engross ourselves with the idea of living for the moment so much that the future gets ignored, but should instead experience each tick of the clock that makes up today; tell our loved ones, "I love you" today; call the friend we've been meaning to call for a long time and say, "Hello" today.

The Buddhist Principle about past, future and present surfaced in my mind.

It was soothing to feel the cool evening wind on my face because my head got heated from all of that thinking. I looked up and saw that the clouds cleared and blue sky was visible. Golden rays of evening sun filtered between the fluttering green leaves of tall poplars in my backyard. At that precise moment, they appeared to me like rays of spiritual enlightenment. Soon it would be dusk but I knew that it was the dawn of a new way of life for me.

I got out of the chair, walked briskly into my house and saw my wife in the kitchen. I embraced her fondly and said, "I love you very much, Honey."

She wore an expression of pleasant surprise and asked softly, "What was that all about?"

I just smiled and said nothing. I simply held her close. I

felt very good in my heart, peaceful and calm in my mind, like the calm after the storm, like the calm of very early morning on a beautiful new day.

*   *   *

**"Yesterday is ashes; tomorrow wood.
Only today does the fire burn brightly."**

—Eskimo saying

"Some people are making such
thorough preparation for rainy days that
they are not enjoying today's sunshine."

—William Feather

Tomorrow May Not Be the Same

I kept staring at the small area of brain exposed through the opening in the skull, pinkish, soft and pulsatile tissue that made us what we were, our personalities, ideas and desires. Every time I looked at the brain, I experienced the awe and respect it deserved.

I was a fourth-year neurosurgery resident at that time, assisting one of my attending surgeons remove a brain tumor from a patient. A small piece of the tumor was taken out and had been sent, a few minutes earlier, to the pathology department for frozen section biopsy.

My reverie was broken by a crackling voice from the intercom. It was the pathologist giving us the biopsy report. "Undifferentiated carcinoma," his voice said.

Those were the words you did not want to hear. Words that were harbingers of a very sad prognosis, words that rung a death knell.

I distinctly remember, even now, seven years later, the sinking feeling in the pit of my stomach when I heard those devastating words. That feeling was awful and unforgettable and I felt such profound sympathy for the patient.

His name was Anil.

He was just 32 years old, much too young to have a problem like the one that was just diagnosed, a rapidly progressing cancer that spread to his brain, originating somewhere else in the body.

Many thoughts swirled in my mind for a moment that felt like eternity. I was not sure if I wanted to be around Anil and his family when he would come to know the diagnosis for the first time. It would be shocking and unbearable.

I pictured the terrified expression on his face. The thought that Anil might not have anticipated that something like a brain tumor would ever happen to him, especially at a very young age, was hard to accept. The sudden realization that his life was going to end in possibly a matter of months was depressing.

I felt an urge to put my hand on Anil's shoulder and say everything would be alright (which really wasn't the truth), but all I could see was the small area of brain that was being operated upon, surrounded by sterile drapes that completely covered the rest of Anil, anesthetized and oblivious of the profoundly emotional reality unfolding around him.

Tomorrow would never be the same.

I had to make a conscious effort to concentrate on assisting my attending surgeon and not allow my thoughts to linger on Anil's situation of impending misery and suffering. I must say it was somewhat difficult to do.

As I was walking along Anil's bed on the way to the intensive care unit, after surgery was done, I thought about our first meeting.

I met Anil two days prior to the day of his surgery. He was admitted in the neurosurgery ward. I was the resident responsible for taking care of his history, physical exam and lab work to get him ready for the surgery.

It was around 4 p.m. when I first walked into Anil's room. He was lying in bed, eyes closed and quiet. His wife, I supposed, was sitting in a chair next to his bed, holding his hand. She had a somber expression on her face, as if she had an intuition that something might go terribly wrong.

"Hello, I am Dr. Palavali, one of the neurosurgery residents."

Anil slowly opened his eyes and sat up in the bed. I extended my hand to shake his. He calmly extended his hand and shook mine. "I am Anil, Doctor, and this is my wife." It looked like he was trying to smile but his expression was one of fear, hope and sadness, all mixed in one.

I pulled a chair next to his bed and sat down, while greeting his wife. "I am here to do a history and physical exam," I said. He nodded his head as if he had been expecting me.

"How are you doing today?" I asked, before getting detailed information about his symptoms. There was a short period of silence.

"Uh…" he was somewhat hesitant before he continued, unsure of how he really was feeling, "Alright … I suppose," he answered unsteadily. I thought I saw his eyes glisten with a film of tears. He must have had a suspicion that the tumor in his brain could turn his life completely upside down.

I looked at his wife whose eyes looked equally sad. The pain in their faces was beginning to make me feel a little uneasy. I felt like completing the H & P as soon as possible and getting out of the room.

"Could you briefly tell me how your problem started and what has been done so far?" I asked. Anil started talking slowly in a monotonous voice that sporadically choked with emotion.

Through our conversation, I came to know that he was an engineer, married with two boys. His main problem was "just some headaches" that started a couple of months ago. Initially they would come and go; of late they had gotten more frequent and severe. He thought they might have been due to refractory error of his eyes or the stress of working a lot of overtime. He said he was working extra hours because he was in the process of buying a house and could use the money.

He had his eyes examined by an ophthalmologist and was told that there was no problem with them. The eye doctor wanted to make sure that there was no problem in his brain causing headaches and ordered a CAT scan a few days ago.

"I was shocked when the ophthalmologist told me that there was a tumor in my brain," the words fading away somewhat towards the end of the sentence as if it were unbearable for him to actually say this. He looked away from me briefly, trying to compose himself.

I myself had difficulty looking them straight in the eyes. I looked down and scribbled some notes. Anil continued.

"He told me that I needed to consult a brain surgeon and I saw one a few days ago," he paused a little and then went on. "The neurosurgeon told me that I needed surgery to remove the tumor to take the pressure off the brain and also to find out exactly what kind of tumor it is."

His lips trembled a little when he said, "I hope it's not cancer, Doc." He could not talk further and put his hands on his face to prevent me from seeing the tears that began to roll down his cheeks.

I glanced at his wife who was tearful, too. Before I could decide what to do next, Anil took his hands off his face and continued to talk. He did not make any effort to hide his tears anymore. He had to get all of his emotions out.

"I'm scared, Doctor. I don't know what to do if it turns out to be cancer. I'm very concerned about my wife and my two boys."

"Anil, don't worry about us," his wife said, wiping tears off her cheeks.

"I can't help but worry about my family, Doctor! I don't know how long I have if it's cancer," he said, looking straight into my eyes.

I fumbled for some reassuring words and said, "We don't know what it is yet. Let's hope it's not going to be cancer." I tried to sound hopeful but I knew, based on the way the tumor looked on the MRI scans, it was very likely to be cancer.

Throughout the rest of H&P, he was very anxious to get answers to many questions that he had. It was as if he were thinking aloud and expressing his fears and concerns. It must have been cathartic.

He asked me, in the case of cancer, if he would need radiation or chemotherapy. He kept talking about how, if he did not have much time to live, he should do something about the future of his lovely wife and the two wonderful boys. He said he saved enough money after working hard for a long time and recently put down payment on a beautiful house that they were going to close on in two weeks. He was very concerned that it might not be realized. He said that he worked very hard all his life at the expense of spending time with his family, not doing many of the things he always wanted to do. He was finally beginning to feel that he might be settling down and was looking forward to enjoying the new house. In fact, he was planning on slowing down to spend more time with his family.

At one point he chuckled ironically and said, "Doc, I thought I waited so long and finally reached a point in my life where I would have peace of mind." He paused briefly then continued, "But with the possibility of having cancer, peace of mind is the last thing I have."

It was very hard for me to come up with answers for any of his questions. All I could say was that until we did surgery and sent a piece of the tumor to pathology, we would not know for sure what it was. I told him it could turn out to be something treatable.

I came back to the present as I reached the intensive care unit. My suspicion of cancer in his brain proved to be correct. I deliberately avoided looking at Anil's face for fear that he would ask me what the diagnosis was.

I did not want to be the one to give him the news that he had brain cancer.

As I was walking home from the hospital that evening, the unfortunate turn of events in Anil's life kept coming back to me. I could not help but wonder how his wife and two boys would be able to handle their lives without Anil. All the dreams and plans he had meant nothing anymore. He would not be alive to enjoy them. I thought about how his family would miss him whenever they felt like sharing the happy moments and shouldering the burdens. I remembered his words about how he waited so long, at the expense of little pleasures in life, to reach a point when his dreams were about to be realized.

They wouldn't be.

Whatever short period of his life was left would be spent with impending mortality looming over his head. Their lives would never be the same. In fact, tomorrow would be depressingly different. I knew Anil would do anything to be able to prevent the cancer from consuming him.

At that moment it occurred to me that I was fortunate to not have any health problems. I realized that there was no reason for me to complain about anything in my life at all, as long as I was healthy. Just the fact that I was alive was enough to celebrate each and every moment.

Something happened to me then. Suddenly the evening

breeze on my face felt wonderful, the chirping of birds sounded musical, the gentle swaying of the trees looked lively, the kids playing in the streets seemed joyful and the brilliant colors of the evening sky appeared spectacular.

Just the recognition of my well-being made me feel that everything around me was simply beautiful.

Over the next few days of Anil's hospital stay, until his discharge, I felt sad every time I saw him, especially after he was told about his diagnosis. I would never forget the melancholic expression on his face.

I learned later that Anil died after ten months. I could not stop thinking about his two young boys. Anil's ordeal would always be part of my memory, for it affected and influenced how I live my life. It made me realize not to put off living for a convenient time in the future, a future that might not be the way you wished it to be. It made me not ignore the simple pleasures of life. Life could change in an instant in such a way that one might not have the body or mind to relish even the simplest things. During the summers of my residency I used to look out through the windows of my apartment onto Lake Michigan, and see all the sailing boats and wish I could sail, too. The first day after my residency I took up lessons in sailing. I also got certified in scuba diving, another interest that I wanted to fulfill for quite some time. As soon as I started my private practice, my wife and I did not waste any time building a house the way we wanted. We had no valid reason to procrastinate on any of those things. When I was young I wanted to show my parents a few places in the world. It was very satisfying to recently fulfill that wish and to be able to express my love and respect for them and my appreciation for all the sacrifices they made for me. I was fortunate to have the time, health and resources to be able to do that.

I now have a tremendous sense of peace of mind. I live a balanced life as far as my work and my family life are concerned. I enjoy my time with my wife and my two boys as much as I can and I love being in the operating room performing surgery. Seeing situations like Anil's has taught me to go after my wishes and dreams today rather than waiting for a distant and uncertain future. Because tomorrow may not be the same.

*   *   *

"Happy are those whose life is today."

—Aji Kwei Armah

> "Life is always a story of atoms coming together and then, eventually, dispersing again...so long as we exist, death is not, and when death is, we are not...Death is nothing to us."
>
> —Epicurus

Love of Life

It was a beautiful evening.

The sun was just setting in the horizon over bluish gray waters of the tropical ocean. It was a spectacular, large and perfectly round reddish orange ball, which never stops mesmerizing me, no matter how many times I watch it.

The sea breeze was beginning to cool down and felt pleasant on my face. A sailboat was lazily moving across the waters, in step with the unhurried island life. My wife was watching the sunset, too, and my two boys, six and two years old, were playing in the sand on the beach, letting fistfuls of sand slip through their fingers. Bare feet, sand, shells and water, a perfect combination for my boys—and for their father! It was like paradise; one of those moments that captured the essence of everything I feel about life itself.

Life!

It is marvelous. It is joyful and exhilarating at times, wonderful most of the time. Of course, it can also be sorrowful. It can be calm, serene and sedate, like that evening, but it sure can be noisy and confusing, too. To me, though, it is just simply beautiful.

I must say, though, that my deep appreciation for life did not happen overnight. The path to this philosophical understanding/destination has been tortuous, with detours of uncertainty, despair, fear and even depression, fortunately only once and transient. But, the journey has been well worth it.

Ironically, that journey (I wonder if I could call it my spiritual journey) began with a sudden preoccupation during my teenage years with (you are not going to believe this) death, which is quite the opposite of life.

Death.

It is a terrifying thought.

I realize, now, that it was not death that bothered me, but rather the fear of death, for once you are dead, you are dead. You won't be feeling or thinking a thing after death. It is when you are alive that the thought of death is excruciating. The thought alone will not kill you, but it can torture you, slowly and intermittently but sometimes incessantly. I say that out of personal experience.

I will never forget the moment the dreadful thought of my mortality sprang into my mind, out of nowhere. I remember the exact feelings I experienced: a chilling sensation, a sense of loneliness, hopelessness and inexplicable fear followed by depression. It made me dread being alone. I needed to see somebody, anybody, to get some comfort by knowing that I was not alone. I had to do everything in my power to keep my mind occupied and distracted, otherwise the thought would creep into my consciousness. The worst part of it all was that the thought was not fleeting. It haunted me, not for a day or two, or a month or two, but for a whole year.

I was sixteen years old, growing up in India.

I wanted to run away from the thought of it, if there were a way to do so. But I don't think anybody can. One's mind is like one's shadow on a sunny day; you just cannot get away from it. As Khalil Gibran said, "Your mind is a dutiful servant if you control it, but an excruciating master if you let it control you."

Needless to say, my uncontrollable preoccupation with death made me restless and unhappy, not the way a sixteen year old should be. My friends were busy thinking about girls while I was trying, during most of my waking moments, to submerge the thought of death. Even girls didn't do the trick.

I guess I didn't like the idea of dying. Not many people do. I wished for eternal life. I questioned why we have to die.

I felt it was unfair. Life is good. No! Life is damn good and then you die. I remember, before being gripped with the thought of death, that I had been carefree. I was looking forward to future, had dreamt about it and, in a way, predominantly lived for the future until that day when my mind was seized with my own mortality. There was no context. Nobody in my family was ill or had died. The thought just happened. I know I have an inquisitive mind, but I did not intentionally go searching for answers about the end of my existence.

Eventually, a year later, my savior was a small story called *The Law of Life*. It was in a book titled *To Build a Fire,* by Jack London. I came across the book in my father's library accidentally, but fortunately. It is about the death of an old, blind Eskimo man, left behind by his son before he moved to a different place in search of food. It was their custom to leave any unnecessary and burdensome objects behind to make their nomadic way of life easy and practical. An old, blind man was not of much use and is big burden on the limited and precious supply of food. The son was nice enough to leave a sizable ration of food for his father. As the old man remembers doing the same thing to his father and appreciates his son's generosity, he feels something wet on his hand and realizes that it is a wolf licking him. He drives it away, only to be surrounded by a pack of wolves within a short time. Soon he realizes that it would be a futile fight and gives up against the pack of wolves. He accepts death as "the law of life" and his time has come.

That short but dramatic story made me accept death as an inescapable reality. There was no point in fighting that thought.

I still do not like death, but by accepting its inevitability, I now have peace of mind. That is exactly what Dalai Lama said.

He explains that death is actually a part of our lives, something that is bound to happen. Since it is inevitable, it makes more sense to try to understand death instead of avoiding thinking about it. The Dali Lama believes that we all have the same body and so we will all die, but from the beginning our attitude should be one of acceptance: "You have to think about and accept death in order not to be terrified by it." Boy, do I know exactly what he means! Some may have difficulty accepting that finality. We may have to be careful not to be too consumed by the idea of death. There is a danger that we may be overcome with despair if our thoughts dwell on the exquisite and final truth of death, especially if one's life is miserable. No wonder some may even give up because they feel there is no point. It is hard to go on with daily life thinking about the reality that, in the end, all of this won't matter. But it does matter, right now.

Twenty-eight years have passed and I still do not have any idea what brought on that thought that horrified me for a whole year, but now I do not think much about death. Instead, I think about life, the beauty, pleasure, wonder and magnificence of it. Occasionally I am faced with that final darkness, especially with encounters and experiences like those with Brad and Anil; but I am not terrified anymore of my own eventual mortality. The awareness of inescapable finality has been transformed into a healthy inspiration and a sense of urgency to celebrate my life before I die. It is what Brad and Anil would have done if given another chance.

*　　　*　　　*

"Fear not that your life shall come to an end, but rather fear that it never has a beginning."

—Cardinal Neumann

Everything is extraordinarily clear. I see the whole landscape before me, I see my hands, my feet, my toes and I smell the rich river mud. I feel a sense of tremendous strangeness and wonder at being alive. Wonder of wonders.

—The Buddha

Stroll in the Sand

The sun was up an hour or so ago. Both my boys and I were walking on the beach towards the water. I was walking barefoot. I wanted to. I do not get to do that much anymore, though I used to go barefoot more when I was growing up in India. I had almost forgotten how good it felt to walk outside

41

and feel the earth on my bare soles. My feet sank into the sand with each step, burying my toes momentarily. The sand was not too warm yet, it was not too cool, either; just the perfect temperature. I knew it would get hot in a few hours. But for now it was pleasant and reminded me of my younger days.

As we reached the water my sons ran in, no hesitation. I was not sure if the water was cold so I tested it with my toe. It was a little cold. I guess it did not bother my boys who were more than happy just to get wet. I am sure I was just like them when I was their age, more spontaneous. Becoming an adult makes you too precautionary, which kills spontaneity. I read somewhere that we should not forget how to be a child. I guess we should be vigilant of transforming ourselves into too much of a grown-up. It is very easy to get too involved in adult responsibilities, distracted from simple pleasures and fun in life, like jumping into the water without waiting to check its temperature first.

I stepped into the water. Within a few seconds, it did not feel cold anymore. I could feel the waves caressing my feet. I wondered how many miles into the ocean the wave began its journey before breaking around my ankle. There was a rhythm to the ebb and flow of the waves. As the wave receded back into the sea it took along with it some of the sand from underneath me and I could feel myself sinking down a little bit only to be lifted up again by the next incoming wave. It was as if the earth and ocean were rocking me to let go of all my worries and concerns. I felt very close and connected to this earth. After all, I am a part of it. I should do this more often.

My son called me to look at the red crab that got washed onto a nearby rock. It was beautiful and glistening, the sun lighting up its brilliant red. The crab hurried back towards the water. It made me smile to look at it scurrying sideways. I looked up at the beach and felt like taking a stroll. I called my boys to see if they were interested in walking along the beach. They didn't even raise their heads; they were simply mesmerized by the crab. I told them that they might find more crabs further up the beach. That perked their interest.

As we were strolling up the beach, leisurely, I liked the way it felt. Like life had slowed down to a perfect pace. Usually around that time I am in my car racing to go to work. Yes, cars are convenient and comfortable but the downside to speed is that life becomes too busy and too fast, just not enough walking. Then, all of a sudden, I realized the sheer pleasure I was getting from the stroll in the sand. Nothing fancy, expensive or complicated, just simple barefoot walking. What a pleasure and joy! I wondered how many of us take walking for granted because we are too busy and have become oblivious to its pleasures. At that moment, something made me stop for a second. It was the thought of all the people who want to but can not walk.

And I was immediately reminded of Daryl. I bet he would do anything to be able to take just a few simple steps.

*   *   *

"The secret of health for both mind and body is not to mourn for the past, nor to worry about the future, but to live the present moment wisely and earnestly."

—Buddha

> "All the wonderful things in life are so simple
> that one is not aware of their wonder
> until they are beyond touch."
>
> —Frances Gunther

Walk While You Can

It was a busy Tuesday. I was seeing patients in the outpatient clinic, hurrying from exam room to exam room, getting impatient and slightly irritable for being a little behind schedule. I walked out of one of the rooms, turned briskly in the corridor to go to the next one and stopped, abruptly, when I recognized the patient my secretary was bringing. I just stood there, motionless, looking at him for a short time while many different emotions whirled through my mind. He was well-built, young and handsome but appeared melancholic, his head slightly slumped down. He was gazing at the floor, indifferent to his surroundings. I did not know what to say right away. It was incongruous to see such a young, seemingly strong and healthy man being wheeled in a wheel chair.

His suffering started four weeks ago.

It was a still and crisp autumn evening. I just walked out of the main entrance of the hospital. The sky was purple and pink as the sun was setting. The cool, fresh evening air of a Michigan autumn felt invigorating on my face, especially after a whole day of being in operating room with a mask on my nose. I took a long, deep breath and was enjoying the air in my lungs, when my beeper went off. I recognized the ER phone number. I let out a long sigh and instead of walking towards my car, turned around and proceeded back in.

The trauma surgeon met me in the ER.

"Hi, Dr. Palavali," he said.

"Hi, Mark, what's going on?" I asked.

"We have a 21-year old African-American man shot in the back. He is completely paralyzed from the waist down."

My head shook from side to side, in disbelief and pity for the young man that I had not even seen yet, for his chances of ever walking again were very likely to be slim to none. No matter how long I had been in neurosurgical practice, the situation of a young person with sudden paralysis of the arms or legs never failed to bring on deep emotion in me. I could feel the sadness hanging like a cloud in my mind, as I listened to Mark continuing about the patient's neurological condition.

"He has no sensation from his umbilicus down and his legs have no movement at all. His rectal tone is flaccid."

As we walked into the adjacent room where the patient was, I asked Mark what the patient's name was. His name was Daryl. The paramedics brought him in an ambulance. He was laying on a stretcher in one of the trauma bays of the ER. He was holding his right thigh with both of his hands, as if trying to move his paralyzed leg. His eyes were red and I could not miss the expression of shock and fear on his face.

"Hi, Daryl, I am Dr. Palavali, one of the neurosurgeons here." I was careful not to ask how he was doing. I was certain that he was utterly frightened at the prospect of possibly not being able to walk again.

He looked right into my eyes. For a moment, I thought I saw in his face what looked like a glimmer of hope that I could fix his spine and make him walk.

"Doc, do you think I will walk again?" were the very first words that came out of his mouth. His lips quivered as he asked that question. I did not expect such a direct, disturbing question right away.

Fear, hope, sadness and uncertainty. I saw all of it in his face as he continued to look into my eyes. The gaze was pitiful but felt piercing to me and made me somewhat uneasy. I could not answer him right away.

"Well..." I was searching for the most appropriate words (if there were ever any under these circumstances) to phrase my reply to such an intense and emotionally delicate question. I was sure that the only answer he wished to hear from me was that he would walk again.

"Doc, please tell me I can." This time he was very anxious.

I perfectly understood his anxiety in expecting an answer immediately but, first of all, I had to examine him and then review all his spine x-rays and CT scan before having any reasonable idea of how badly his spine was damaged and if he would be able to ever walk again.

"Well, I have to examine you and look at all the x-rays before I can answer that question, Daryl."

He sighed as if he could not bear to wait any to know what his fate was going to be. But he nodded his head silently to acknowledge that he understood the necessity for the examination.

I waited for a few seconds and asked, "How did this happen, Daryl?"

He buried his face in his hands for a moment. Then he looked up and started talking.

"I went to get some things in the convenience store near my house, Doc. I just got out of the store and saw my friend. I was just standing outside the store talking to him. There were a bunch of guys just a few yards from me. This car came real fast and I saw a guy start shooting from the car. My friend and I turned and started to run away. I was running..." He choked a little bit, waited and then continued. "I was running and suddenly felt severe pain in my back. I fell down on the ground. I..., I..."

He paused, as if he could not bear to talk about what happened to him or to accept that it was real. His mouth was trembling slightly. I was listening to him quietly, my hands folded in front of my chest. He composed himself and continued, "I could not feel my legs. I tried to get up and run but could not move my legs at all."

Daryl stopped talking. His eyes were wide open, pupils dilated with an expression of fear from reliving the shooting all over again. He resumed talking.

"My friend was screaming at me to get up and run. He tried to come back but had to run because they kept shooting. I tried to get up on my hands but couldn't. My legs wouldn't move. I tried to pick up my legs with my hands. I could see that I was holding my legs but could not feel the legs at all. I was very scared and could feel my heart in my throat. I thought I was gonna die. I tried to crawl and drag my legs." He paused again.

The image of Daryl crawling on the ground, frantically struggling to get up and run, flashed violently into my mind.

He continued, "The car drove off and the gunshots stopped. My friend came back. He tried to pull me up but my legs were not moving at all. He didn't know what to do. He ran into the store and called 911."

I could see his heart beating faster on the EKG monitor. I could imagine how terrifying it must have been to be lying on the ground, utterly helpless, while bullets were whizzing by.

Daryl continued to talk, "The ambulance picked me up. On the ride to the hospital I kept telling myself that everything would be all right. I would be able to move my legs again any second. I kept touching them but they still couldn't feel or move at all. The thought that I might never walk again came to my mind. I prayed to God to help me move my legs, to help me get up and walk." There was a pause. He looked directly into my eyes and asked again, "Doc, do you think I will?"

I couldn't answer yet, but I knew in my mind that if the bullet went through his spinal cord, Daryl would never walk again.

I put on a pair of gloves and started to examine him. I saw the bullet entry wound in the left flank; approximately a centimeter-sized hole in the skin, its appearance deceptive of the extent of devastation caused in the bullet's path. He had

49

absolutely no nerve function from just below his navel. He could neither move his legs nor feel any touch or pain. His rectal exam showed the anal sphincter to be flaccid, which meant he probably would not be able to control his bowel and bladder function. There was a possibility that he was in spinal shock, which might take a day or two to wear off. Then he might recover some sensation or movement of his legs, but chances weren't good.

"I am going to look at x-rays of your spine. I'll be right back to talk to you," I told Daryl, while peeling off the examination gloves. He simply nodded his head.

I walked silently to the CT scanner room in the ER. The CT scan of his spine was on the viewing box. I could see that, around the lower part of the chest spine, the bullet had shattered the vertebra by entering from the side and was lodged right smack in the middle of the spinal canal where the spinal cord, which controls everything below that level, was located. There were some pieces of bone next to the bullet. I was certain that the spinal cord was completely severed and there was no way it could be repaired.

Daryl would be completely paralyzed from his waist down for the rest of his life.

Telling him that news was not going to be easy. How could I shatter the last hope that he was holding onto? Just a few words would cause unimaginable anguish. Unfortunately, they told the truth.

I went back to talk to Daryl. It was hard to look directly into his eyes and tell him what I truly thought.

"Daryl..." I paused and searched for words.

"Daryl, I am afraid I don't have any good news for you."

I could see the expression in his face change instantly to disappointment mixed with fear.

"The spinal cord is damaged really badly in your spine. There is no surgery that I could do to fix it."

"Does that mean I can't walk, ever again?" He started to shake.

"If in the next few days there is any significant movement of your legs, that would be good news. There is a small possibility that the spinal cord may be in shock and you may regain some function. I don't know if that is going to be enough to walk or not. We will have to just wait and see."

Daryl shook his head, not wanting to hear those words. But I continued.

"The chances of that happening are extremely small. I…I am afraid the situation doesn't look good. You are going to need lot of rehabilitation for a prolonged period."

I had to add that so that he would not have any hopes that would turn out to be untrue.

The disbelief on his face could not be missed. He probably had high hopes that, as a neurosurgeon, I could make him walk, until I shattered them with my prognosis. There were some injuries that could be fixed with surgery and many that could not.

"You will be admitted in the neuro unit and observed."

He was just staring at me, as if he were in psychological shock.

"I am very sorry, Daryl."

I saw a tear roll down his cheek. He let his head hang down and covered his face with his hands. He did not say anything. I waited a short while, awkwardly.

"Is your family here?"

He was quiet.

"They are in the conference room, Doctor," the trauma PA told me.

Suddenly Daryl lifted his head, looked at me and said, "Doc, I am going to walk again." His expression was grim but determined. "I'm going to do everything I can and hope God will help me."

I put my hand on his shoulder gently and said, "I hope so too, Daryl."

Daryl did not say anything further. In that situation I would not know what to say, either.

"I will be checking on you every day." I patted his shoulder.

Silence.

"I'm going to talk to your dad and mom." I took his hand into mine and told him, "Hang in there."

I turned around and headed for the door. After I left him, I had thoughts of how his life was going to be drastically altered. Even though I knew that his chances of walking were slim, I wished he would fall in that extremely small percentage of patients who might have enough residual function of the spinal cord to allow some movement of the legs, enough to use a walker or crutches. I knew that I was being unrealistically optimistic, but when I saw how young he was I could not help but feel that way. It especially broke my heart when I came to know that he had nothing to do with the shooting and was an innocent bystander. He was a good young man who would probably spend the rest of his life in a wheel chair for being at the wrong place at the wrong moment.

His mom and dad were in the conference room with the

social worker. It was very hard to inform them that their only son might never walk again. I will never forget his mother's face at that moment. There was also a good possibility that Daryl would become depressed. The whole ordeal was going to be hard on his family as well, but he was going to need their support more than ever.

While in the hospital, Daryl never regained any voluntary movement of his legs. The sensation in his lower body did not return, either. He had a catheter in his urinary bladder initially, which was taken out a few days later to prevent infection. He had no control of his bladder and was taught to insert the catheter himself, intermittently, to drain urine. He had no control of his bowels, either.

A few days later he was gradually helped out of bed and sat up in a chair. It was two weeks since he became paralyzed. He would be transferred to the rehab unit and would eventually go home in a wheelchair.

It was heart-wrenching to watch Daryl's initial hope gradually fade and make way for the frightening reality that he would never walk again. Over a few days he became withdrawn. He would not interact much with anybody. He was just lying in bed most of the time with his eyes closed, since opening them would force him to look at his legs. I could imagine him battling, in his mind, with the terrible reality of his future, a future of being confined to a wheel chair, not being able to stand without somebody holding him. The times he was running, playing without a care and simply walking to school must now be painful memories. I could not imagine how hard it must be to think of walking, which we take for granted, as a mere memory.

I wondered how many times he must have asked himself, "Why me? How did this happen? What if I were not at that place, at that moment?" There were no answers for any of those questions. Even if there were, it would not make any difference now. It would not bring back a life of careless running, playing and walking.

The last day I visited Daryl in the hospital, I saw that he kept touching his legs to see if he had any sensation. He stopped after awhile and asked, for the last time, "I'll never walk again, will I, Doc?"

One of the hardest questions a neurosurgeon could be asked.

"I'm afraid the chances are slim to none, Daryl."

I could not flat out say, "No," even though that was going to be his fate. I had to pull my gaze away from his teary eyes and looked towards his legs. They were very still. Strong and muscular legs but devoid of any movement. What a paradox! Strong and muscular but, for all practical purposes, dead.

I looked at the wall across from his bed and saw a picture of him standing next to a hoop with a basketball in his hands. How could one cope with such an unimaginable alteration of life? Daryl seemed severely depressed to me.

I was jolted back to the present in the outpatient clinic when my secretary said, "Excuse me, Doctor." Something happened in my mind at that instant. Suddenly I was not hurrying anymore. I was neither impatient nor irritable. It was as if that jolt back to reality brought me some sensibility and perspective. Why had I been upset for being behind schedule? Even if I were delayed significantly, the inconvenience was still insignificant. Daryl's situation was significant; in fact, it was an ordeal. I felt silly that I had let such a small thing like being behind schedule get to me when I had many more important things to be happy about.

That was a moment of profound realization.

I looked at Daryl and said, "Hi, Daryl."

I could not bring myself to ask how he was doing. He did not have to tell me how he was doing. I did not have any difficulty in comprehending. Daryl slowly lifted his head, looked at me and let his head hang down again.

That said it all.

That evening I went home and the image of Daryl in that wheelchair came to mind as I was taking off my shoes. It was a sad reminder. I took my socks off, too. Instead of walking into my bedroom like usual, I silently slipped out to my backyard. I did not know what made me do that. It was as if some subconscious and primitive desire in my mind was automatically directing my legs, probably a desire to just walk. I felt the grass and leaves under my bare feet. I cannot express the pleasure and sense of well being that I experienced as I just wandered aimlessly in my backyard, exquisitely aware of the softness of the grass under my bare feet; perhaps it was a sense of gratitude.

We often take our health for granted and the fact that we don't have any physical limitations. How come we do not use all we've got to the fullest potential? I wondered why I was always on the run or driving around in the car most of the time. There were weeks that went by without me taking a slow, deliberate pleasure walk, like the one I was enjoying at that moment.

It was not only a walk of pleasure but also was of introspection. I remembered a patient who became suddenly paralyzed when his neck broke from a bizarre accident. He was trimming the branches of a tree in his backyard when a branch landed with force on the back of his head and bent his neck forward, severely fracturing his spine. In fact, a couple of years later, the exact same incident caused devastating paralysis in another man. No! I should not take the walks for granted. I swore that I would make every effort to take a walk outside, whenever I could, just because I could, if for no other reason.

* * *

**"What your mind possesses
the body expresses."**

—Anonymous

There is no vocabulary for the love within a family, love that's lived in but not looked at, love within the light of which all else is seen.

—T.S. Eliot

Love of Family

It was about two months since I started my neurosurgery practice, having completed residency training just three months ago. I was going through a pile of mail at the end of the day. It had been a long day. I was anxious to get out of the office and go home as soon as possible. You see, I had a newborn at home, a two-week old boy. I loved going home and holding him in my arms. We named him Neal Akash, which means "blue sky." He sure was like a slice of blue sky in my wife's and my life. He was our first child.

As I was thinking about Neal I started to throw the junk mail faster and faster into the trash can until I saw an envelope with what looked like a greeting card inside. It came from Chicago, where I trained as a neurosurgeon. I could not immediately recognize the sender's address and that sparked my curiosity. I opened the envelope. It was not a greeting card but a funeral announcement card. I flipped it open and looked inside. It was the announcement of Michael's death.

There was a P.S. note at the bottom which read, "Dear Dr. Palavali, Thank you for all your care and kindness. We are very grateful to you." It was signed by Michael's wife and mother.

Instantly Michael's ordeal, spanning close to two years, played back in my mind as I stood there with the card in my hand and sadness in my heart.

I first met Mike when I was a fourth-year resident on call. Dr. Moller (Mike's surgeon) called me and told me to meet Mike at the MRI suite to have an urgent MRI done on his neck spine. Mike apparently was complaining of progressive weakness of his arms and legs in the past few weeks.

When I met Mike, I got the instant impression that he was a very nice guy. He was 36 years old, tall, gentle and quiet. As we talked, I found out that he unfortunately had a tumor called chordoma. The tumor was located at part of the base of his skull called the clivus, near the junction of his skull and neck spine in front of the spinal cord, compressing it. The location made it difficult to completely remove the tumor through surgery. It was not very responsive to radiation therapy, either. In fact he already had surgery twice; the first one was from the side of the neck and head to remove as much of the tumor as possible and the second one from the back of the neck to stabilize the spine with wires and bone. The last surgery was a year and half ago. He was doing well until a few weeks ago when he noticed that it was getting difficult to walk and to raise his arms.

As soon as the MRI was done I compared it to the old MRI done soon after the previous surgery. Unfortunately the tumor grew in size and was compressing the spinal cord significantly, causing the weakness of the arms and legs. Since he already had radiation and the tumor was not very responsive, the only option he had was to undergo surgery again. It was just one of many more surgeries yet to come.

I came into the waiting room where Mike and his wife were sitting.

"What does the MRI show, Doc?" Mike asked.

I looked at them and replied slowly, "I am sorry to say that the tumor has grown in size and is putting pressure on your spinal cord."

You could not miss the disappointment on their faces. They immediately looked at each other, knowing that it meant more surgery. Mike's wife put her hand on his arm, showing that she was there for him. I hesitated to continue.

"So that's what's causing my weakness," Mike said with a sad tone.

I empathized with his situation and could not immediately say much, simply nodding my head to agree with his understanding. Nobody talked for a few moments. Mike just sat in the chair with his head down. Then he looked at me and asked, "When do we do the surgery, Doc?"

"I will have to talk to Dr. Moller. I'm sure he'll want to do it as soon as possible and I think he'll want you to get admitted in the hospital right away."

Mike shook his head side to side. I could not understand if he meant that he was not going to or something else.

"I told my son that I would take him to the ball game tomorrow. Do you think it can wait a couple of days before I go to the hospital?"

"Mike! We need to take care of this first," his wife said.

I nodded my head in agreement. "I am very sorry, Mike. I agree with her but I know how you feel." He agreed reluctantly.

Two days later he had surgery. Again the tumor could not be removed completely. Only the part that was pressing on the spinal cord was removed. The tumor will keep coming back more and more frequently and will need to be operated on accordingly. His quality of life will get worse and his suffering more. It was a no-win situation.

I met Mike's mother and his two boys on the day of surgery. The boys were three and six years old, handsome and playing with toy cars in the waiting lounge. They kept asking when they were going to see their father. Their mother and grandmother were doing the best they could to explain what was going on but the boys had no comprehension of the situation. You could tell that they were a loving and close-knit family. I kept thinking about how Mike said he promised to take the boys to the ball game and felt sad to know that there would be a lot more that Mike would not be able to do with his boys in the days to come, for his tumor was going to be aggressive and relentless.

After surgery Mike could not wait to see his boys, wife and mother. He asked for them even before he got to his room.

Over the next week of his stay, I noticed that every time his boys visited, Mike could not wait for them to hop on the bed next to him. His spirits would visibly lift. His family never failed to bring a smile to his face the moment they walked into the room. It was heart-breaking to imagine how devastating it was going to be when one member of such a loving family would gradually suffer more and more, becoming increasingly incapacitated.

Within a week Mike went home with some outpatient rehabilitation arranged for him to improve his strength and walking.

I saw Mike again four months later. Even though his arms and legs got better after surgery, he noticed another weakening in the past few weeks. He seemed quieter and more worried as if he realized he was beginning to fight a losing battle. An MRI showed that the tumor had grown again.

He underwent another surgery but a lot of his strength could not be regained.

The tumor was growing so rapidly that he required surgery almost every month; each time he had less strength because less of the tumor could be removed. In the beginning he was able to go home between surgeries but, as time went by and surgery became weekly, he couldn't. It got to a point where the tumor grew to the skin of his neck so we could not even close the wound after surgery. We had to give up on any further intervention.

I saw him go from walking without assistance to a cane, to a walker, to a wheelchair. Eventually he did not have any movement in his arms and legs and was confined to bed. Throughout Mike's ordeal I never saw his wife and mother give up on him. They were at his bedside every day. But I could see that it was very hard on them to watch what he was going through.

Towards the end of my residency, Mike became completely paralyzed from the neck down, including his respiratory muscles. He could not breathe anymore and needed to be on ventilator support 24 hours a day. The only things he could move were his eyes and lips. He could not talk because the ventilator tube had to be put into his wind pipe (trachea) through a hole in his neck. I remember thinking that I would not wish that kind of suffering even upon my worst enemy. It was, to me, hell on earth. But the most amazing thing was that Mike never once said he wanted to die; neither did the family want to withdraw his life support.

I was impressed by Mike's will to survive and continue in that terrible physical condition. He was completely aware of his agony because the tumor affected everything from his neck down but not his mind. I was not able to explain what made Mike endure such immeasurable suffering, until one day when I went into his room.

I saw Mike lying motionless in bed. His entire body was

swollen, the ventilator tube coming out of the front of his neck. In spite of his condition, there was a twinkle in his eyes looking at his two beautiful boys sitting next to him. They were talking non-stop about something or other. I could not see if he was smiling or not because his face was so swollen, but I was certain that he was. Then it hit me that Mike endured unimaginable agony every minute of his life just to look at his two beautiful boys, his wife and mother. It was the love for his family that gave him the strength to endure hell.

I was in awe of the power of that love.

I completed my residency a few weeks after that and left Chicago to start my practice in Michigan. Not long after that I came to know, while talking to one of the junior residents at Chicago, that Mike died. He was in a coma for a few days before his brain activity completely stopped and he was declared brain dead. Before he went into the coma he gradually became lethargic due to increased pressure in his brain. The tumor in his neck grew very large and obstructed the veins that carry the blood from his brain through the neck to the heart, causing coma and later brain death. When I heard about his death, I was very sad but somewhat consoled that finally, after close to one and a half years of indescribable suffering, there was an end to Mike's agony.

I will always remember how pleasant Mike was and what a loving family he had. But most of all, I will never forget the love in his eyes when he was looking at his boys, even though he could not touch them.

The thought of his boys brought my boy to mind and took me back into the present.

Leaving rest of the mail on my desk, I walked out of my office and briskly to my car. I could not wait to reach my home, for I had an urge to give my wife a hug and to hold my son in my arms.

*   *   *

"The family is one of nature's masterpieces."

—George Santayana

> "Your children are not your children.
> They are sons and daughters of life's
> longing for itself."
>
> —Kahlil Gibran

The Invisible Bond

The surgeon was just about to make the incision on my wife's belly. She was having a cesarean section done, which was not what she originally wanted. She was pregnant with our first child, a boy, and wished for a water delivery if possible, about which I had no idea whatsoever. Since that could not be done, she settled for natural delivery. To this day I still can't believe how she tolerated those contractions. Unfortunately my boy's head was too big to be delivered naturally. My wife was not

65

happy finding that out after 12 long and painful hours of pushing, by which time she had enough of dealing with those labor pains. She couldn't wait to get done with the process of giving birth and agreed to go ahead with a c-section. During those hours of unbearable pain she blamed me for being responsible for making her pregnant, as if she didn't have anything to do with it. But I was not going to argue with her, at that time, about her participation in creating our baby.

She was taken to the operating room and had spinal anesthesia. Then they prepped and draped her belly. I was standing near her head with the video camera in my hand, a sterile drape between me and my wife's belly. I suppose it is implicitly understood that the Dad is the official photographer during the birth. I was about to start shooting the arrival into this world of our first child, when I thought I heard my wife say that she couldn't breathe. I looked at her; she had a panicked expression on her face and said that it was getting harder and harder to breathe and that she couldn't move her arms. The number on the monitor measuring the amount of oxygen in her blood was dropping rapidly. Being a physician myself, I could immediately comprehend that if they didn't put a tube in her lungs to help her breathe, she would have severe problems, including brain damage, from lack of oxygen. The spinal anesthetic that was only supposed to work on the lower half of her body had moved up and was paralyzing her chest and arm muscles. No wonder she couldn't breathe. I looked at the CRNA and told her that my wife needed to be intubated, stat.

There was some tension before the anesthesiologist came into the room and was able to put the tube into my wife's lungs. He felt some relief and must have been taking a breather, letting go of the tube for a moment, something you don't do until it is secured well. The tube came out when my wife coughed and I was standing there thinking, "This is not happening." The anesthesiologist started all over again and this time everything went fine. By the time my wife settled down under general anesthesia and I could relax, the baby was already out and the surgeon was closing the belly. I had only a glimpse of the boy being taken away. I didn't see what he looked like; I was too concerned about my wife. When you are a physician and something is not right, thoughts of the worst possible consequences run through your mind. I was hoping that her brain was not deprived of oxygen for too long because all you need is a few minutes before irreversible brain damage occurs. Needless to say I was very eager for the surgery to be over and for my wife to wake up so I could know that everything was fine, but it would be a while before she came out of the effects of the anesthesia.

When I checked her and found that everything was alright, I could no longer suppress my strong desire to see my son. My little boy was already in the room where they keep the newborn babies. I walked over and saw him for the first time.

I was stunned. He looked like an exact replica of me when I was young. I can't express in words the overwhelming feelings I had at that moment. Words cannot do justice to the very first realization that I was now a father responsible (well, half of the responsibility anyway) for creating another human being that looked just like me. I felt warm deep in my heart and experienced a sense of pride and joy, a sense of wonder and amazement and a sense of belonging and family. He was not doing anything in particular. He had his eyes closed mostly, peeking occasionally and his hands closed into fists. He was probably getting used to the strange sensation of being outside his mother's cozy womb. Yet I cannot explain the happiness he gave me. I don't know if there is any way for anybody to understand and appreciate that moment other than to experience it personally.

I remember a discussion I had with my chief resident when I was a third-year resident at the University of Chicago. Not having my own children at that time, but being a big part of the lives of my sisters' kids as they were growing up and loving them a lot, I thought there was no difference between that and the love of our own children. My chief resident disagreed and told me, as a father, that parents absolutely love their own kids, the extensions of their flesh, more than any others. He also told me that I would know that personally when I have my own kids. At that first experience of calling somebody my own son, I knew exactly what he meant.

I can not fathom the force that binds and bonds us with our children, but it is very special and incredibly powerful and there is no other like it. It makes us sacrifice our pleasure and comfort for their pleasure and comfort, makes us accept their misgivings and makes us love them unconditionally. I am sure we have even heard stories about parents who sacrificed their lives in order to protect the lives of their children. It is an inexplicable bond that brings us immeasurable joy and pleasure from our children without any special effort on their part, other than just being our children. Their smile makes us smile, their cry makes us cry and their laughter makes us laugh. It will make us tolerate an incredible amount of suffering just to see their faces.

It was that invisible bond that united Mike and his boys and sustained him through excruciating pain towards the end of his life. In the midst of despair, that bond was a ray of light and a lifeline.

*   *   *

"Life is a flame that is always burning itself out, but it catches fire again every time a child is born."

—George Bernard Shaw

> "One word frees us of all the weight and pain of life. That word is love."
>
> —Sophocles

Unforgivable

The little girl had her eyes closed. She wouldn't open them to her name. I gently rubbed on her sternum (breast bone) to see if they would open. No, they stayed shut. As much as I hate to cause pain in anybody, especially in young kids, I had to apply a painful stimulus, by pressing firmly but carefully on her nail bed, to see if that would make her open her eyes. There was no response. She was not sleeping; she was in a deep coma. She was 18 months old.

I was just finishing the last of my surgeries when I got paged about the little girl. She was brought to the ER by her mother because she was not breathing. The story, according to her mother, was that the little girl had been sleeping and fell from her bed, around three feet high, onto the hard wood floor. She had a seizure and stopped breathing. But the mother didn't know that her boyfriend, who accompanied her, told a different story to one of the trauma PAs. That's never good! It always raises the possibility of one of the saddest situations that I come across in my life as a brain surgeon. Child abuse!

When she was brought to the ER, the little girl was gasping for air and needed to have a breathing tube put in, connected to a ventilator. She then had a head CT scan and when they noticed some blood on the left side of the brain, they called me for a consultation. By the time I got there, the girl had been transferred to the pediatric ICU and I went there to examine her.

Not only did the little girl not open her eyes, but there was no movement of her arms or legs at all. She was in the deepest coma. I gently lifted her eyelids and shone light on the pupils. There was no response of constriction of the pupil. Her arms and legs were flaccid. She was almost brain dead. The pupils were dilated big enough that I could see the retina in the back of the eye with an ophthalmoscope. There were hemorrhages in the retina, a finding highly indicative of shaking the baby hard, which is usually seen in child abuse injuries. There were also some scars on her body that appeared to be healed cigarette burns. I was sad as well as mad. I could not fathom how anybody could hurt beautiful, innocent and helpless children. I had to calm myself and not let my emotions take me over.

I left the room and went to a nearby conference room to look at the head CT scan on the computer. There was some blood on the brain but that was not her worst problem. There was a stroke of a large part of the left half of her brain from not having enough blood supply. I wondered how it happened. One possibility was that the baby was shaken hard enough that there was a tearing of the lining of a blood vessel in the neck (carotid artery) which in turn blocked the flow of blood to the brain. The other possibility was that there had been hard and prolonged pressure applied on the neck, as if choking, wherein the carotid artery might have been compressed, shutting off blood supply to the brain. The findings on the scan were not consistent with the story of the girl falling from her bed. I was sure that the mother was lying. The girl must have been abused for a while before she eventually reached her present horrible condition. For a second the picture of the baby being shaken violently, while her neck was being choked, popped into my mind. I closed my eyes and shook my head to shake off that horrible image but my anger resurfaced and I felt like my blood was boiling. I opened my eyes and looked at the scan again. The entire brain was swollen, probably from not having enough oxygen. The blood clot itself was not big enough to require any surgery. Lack of oxygen coupled with the stroke were the major problems and surgery was not going to fix either of those. My knowledge, experience and expertise were not going to make any difference.

I came out of the conference room and met the pediatric intensivist taking care of the girl. I told him that there was not much that I could do to help her and that her prognosis was extremely poor. The intensivist nodded his head in agreement.

He told me that he, too, had very high suspicions of child abuse. In fact they were going to x-ray all of her bones to see if any of them were broken, which adds further evidence. Just the thought that that little girl may have experienced untreated and unbearable pain, if there were any broken bones, made me wince inside. He also said that the DCFS (Department of Child and Family Services) was already notified, as required by the law every time child abuse is suspected.

I went to the family waiting room to talk to the mother. When I first saw her I couldn't help but feel some anger and dislike towards her, which subconsciously was affecting my interaction with her. I know I am supposed to be as objective as possible, but I am a human being, too, and am particularly sensitive to the horror of child abuse. I explained about the little girl's critical condition and that she might not survive. There was not much reaction in her face. Her emotions appeared blunt and distant. I couldn't help but wonder if she ever loved the baby in the first place or if she was under the influence of some drug, which was not an unusual assumption. Her boyfriend next to her appeared somewhat impatient. Both were young, maybe in their late twenties.

I left the room after saying what I needed to. During the drive home I could not get over the image of that beautiful little girl being beaten. I always thought that all parents were innately loving towards their children and that the parental bond was strong and unshakable. We keep hearing about a mother's or father's unconditional love, but experiences like these make me wonder. I try very hard to find answers that are acceptable in the face of such cruelty but it is very difficult to come up with any rational explanation. What is it that transforms a loving human being into an inhuman beast inflicting unimaginable pain on helpless children? Is it mental illness or the ills of society? Are the parents themselves subjected to external physical, psychological or social burdens that make them snap under the weight? Are the parents, as well as the children, victims? Is it lack of love or lack of good upbringing or miserable poverty that drives somebody into the uncontrollable clutches of addiction? How responsible is the society that tolerates and, at times, glorifies addiction? Too many questions and not enough answers! And nothing I could do for her, anyway.

I got out of the car and opened the door to my house. My little boy came running into the room, screaming, "Daddy!" In an instant the sadness was replaced by a humbling joy.

At that moment I realized the most important answer to many of my questions.

Love! Yes! Love, individually and collectively as a society, is the answer that can make a difference. It has the power to destroy the conditions that transform humans into beasts. Love has the power to affect our daily actions which, in turn, betters our families, society and the world as a whole. Maybe I am naive to think that way, but it seems to me that, throughout human history, there has always been a battle between self-interest and compassion. Unfortunately, more often than not, self-interest manages to get the upper hand. I am not saying that every one of us has to become Buddha or Dalai Lama or Mother Theresa or Gandhi. But extending a loving hand to the most possible extent, individually and within our personal spheres, can cumulatively make society more compassionate as a whole. I am sure it is easier said than done, but we have to start somewhere. I thought we might as well start with loving our families, especially the innocent, impressionable children, and hope that love will spread beyond our families and connect the peoples of the world as one global community.

I knelt down and hugged my son, who ran into my open arms. It felt so good that I couldn't help but wish that the little girl had that same pleasure. I hugged him a little tighter and longer. I didn't feel like letting go.

*   *   *

"Love children especially, for like angels, they too are sinless and they live to soften and purify our hearts and, as it were, to guide us."

—Fyodor Dostoevsky

> "Faith is the bird that feels the light and sings when the dawn is still dark."
>
> —Rabindranath Tagore

The Power of Faith

His mother found him lying on the floor. There was still a pistol in his right hand, but not much blood around except some that trickled from the bullet hole at his temple. There was a note he had written about his plan to commit suicide. He was motionless with his eyes open, but they were lifeless, as if staring into nothingness. She called his name and shook him to see if he moved. He didn't. She was not sure if he was already dead or still had some life in him. She desperately hoped for any chance to save him. He was only 20 years old.

The mother didn't know how long ago he shot himself. She just walked into the house after buying some groceries and found the boy on the living room floor, next to the chair from which he slid. She called 911. When the paramedics arrived at the house, there were no signs of breathing. They immediately put a tube down his throat into his lungs to help him breathe and brought him to the ER. The ER doctor examined him and didn't find any evidence of obvious brain activity, but he wanted either a neurologist or a neurosurgeon to determine if the patient was brain dead. They did a CAT scan of the brain and found that the bullet shattered the skull at the entry site, went through the entire brain from right to left and got stuck in the skull on the left side. There was a lot of hemorrhaging throughout the bullet track and the entire brain was swollen.

That was the story I got when I was called about the boy. From the details of the ER doctor's neurological examination of him, I had a sense that he was already dead and there was nothing I could do to make any difference. Yet usually the family clings to hope that something could be done by a neurosurgeon. Often with suicidal gun shots to the brain, when the neurosurgeon evaluates the patient's condition, either the patient is brain dead or the damage caused by the bullet traversing a critical part of the brain is so severe that makes it impossible to consider any surgery. In his case, that was exactly the situation.

I went to meet the family, mother, father and two sisters, after I examined the patient and found him brain dead. Needless to say, there were a lot of tears flowing down their faces. We exchanged introductions and the father also introduced a man of the cloth, their priest. I told them the sad truth that the boy was dead. There were more tears and the girls hugged their mother while sobbing uncontrollably. The father, who wept silently, put his hand on his wife's shoulder. The priest in turn put his hand on the father's shoulder. There was stunned, disbelieving silence for a few moments, then the mother asked the priest to pray for her boy. Everybody held one another's hands in a small circle and I was asked to join, too. Knowing what I do about what life and death is all about, I am not a man of prayer but I never refuse if a mourning family asks me pray. The priest said the prayer, mentioning something to the effect that the boy's soul is going to be in heaven, in the presence of God. Afterwards, I told the family that I was sorry I could not help the boy and took leave.

As I was driving home I kept thinking about the priest's words about the soul and heaven. I don't believe in the existence of a soul, at least not the way many people have defined it, as variably as human imagination permits, throughout the past centuries. I have done an extensive dissection of an entire human cadaver during the anatomy course of my medical school and I studied the physiology of the heart and brain but have not found a soul anywhere. Besides the word was not mentioned once anywhere in all the medical text books. As far as heaven is concerned, I have been checking out the pictures of the universe beamed down by the Hubble telescope and have yet to come across a picture of paradise among the stars. Yet, millions of people do believe. And I think I know why.

Situations like that of the young boy who killed himself remind me of the emotional predicaments people face and give me some insight into why we believe the way we do. I don't think I could ever imagine how devastating, horrible and unbearable it must be to face the sudden death of a loved one, especially someone young. Unbearable? Yes, unimaginably unbearable! And how does one cope with such shocking loss? The emotions must be overwhelming and uncontrollable. I can imagine how a tragedy like that can make even a mentally strong person break down from the weight of emotional burden and turmoil. I don't know how I would cope with such a tragedy if I ever had to face one. I hope it never happens to me and I wish that it wouldn't happen to anybody else. But the reality is that there are millions of people facing such unexpected, overwhelming personal tragedies, of different kinds, all the time. Reason and rationality face a daunting task and find it difficult to console the sorrowful heart, at least right away. We all need immediate comforting thoughts and a shoulder to lean on that give us some peace of mind and buy enough time for the emotional wounds to heal. If I understand correctly, the idea of heaven and eternal life offers solace in situations of intolerable and devastating loss, similar to the one that I just witnessed. Somehow faith, even if imagined, is capable of consoling the grieving heart and calming the troubled mind. I think that belief in eternal life in heaven is like after-life insurance. For millions of people, spirituality and faith in the soul, heaven and life after death provide the emotional strength to cope with such tragedies. Considering myself a man of science, I have a hard time accepting such belief but, for many, that belief is essential. If one is a non-believer, one's rationality has to be deep-rooted and unshakable so as to prevent him or her from falling into the abyss of depression or sending the restless and inquisitive mind into a land of insanity.

I suppose a weeping heart settles down and heals faster with a spiritual concept than with a scientific explanation. Besides, mortality is scary and the finality of death can be too hopeless to handle. The concept of heaven and an eternal and happy after-life sure sounds good. That is probably why Pascal said, "Heart knows reasons that reason can not understand." Religious and spiritual faith is very personal and often fulfilling and there is a strong power in faith.

But happiness in this life can create for us a kind of earthly paradise.

*   *   *

"Faith is the strength by which a shattered world shall emerge into the light."

—Helen Keller

> I believe in absolute oneness…and therefore of humanity. What though we have many bodies? We have but one soul.
>
> —Mahatma Gandhi

Sex, Brain and Universal Brotherhood

It was one of the most horrible head injuries I had seen in the 10 years I have been a brain surgeon. The patient was 30 years old. She was up a tree, around 25 feet high, cutting a branch. As the branch fell, it knocked her off and she must have landed right on her head. While in the ER she had a head CT scan done and I could see that the skull was shattered into multiple pieces. There was a large hematoma, called a subdural hematoma, between the brain and its covering. The brain was bruised and swollen. She was in a deep coma when I examined her and had barely minimal brain function. Her prognosis was extremely poor but, because she was not brain dead, I had to operate and remove the subdural hematoma and put in a monitor to keep an eye on the pressure inside her skull. No matter what I did, after surgery, it would still be very likely that the pressure inside her skull was going to be very high and impossible to control. I told the neurosurgery PA to arrange for the patient to be taken to the operating room while I talked to her family about her condition and the need for surgery.

The patient's mother and father were sitting at a table, while another girl, pretty and probably in her late twenties, sat in a chair a few feet away. The girl was visibly shaken, with a terrified expression. Apparently, she actually saw the patient fall and hit the ground. I could imagine how horrifying that must have been. I assumed she was her sister. I introduced myself to the parents and conveyed to them the critical situation their daughter was in. I told them that surgery was necessary to remove the blood clot that was putting pressure on the brain and told them all the possible complications, including the fact that she could die on the operating table. I was candid in discussing the prognosis that, in spite of all our efforts her likelihood of having any meaningful functional recovery was extremely small. On the other hand, her possibility of dying was very high. The parents cried and the girl cried even more. I waited until they were able to control their sorrow to some extent, and asked them if they wanted me to proceed with the surgery.

The parents looked at each other and then at the girl. The mother turned to me, pointed to the girl and said, "Doctor, this is my daughter's partner."

My immediate response was surprise, maybe because I had assumed a totally different relationship between them. I shook her hand gently. The mother continued, "They have been together for many years, Doctor. I think she should make the decision."

I was not really sure how this situation worked. I didn't have a similar experience before and, though I understood that the patient and the girl were living together in a lesbian relationship, I didn't know the legal intricacies of dealing with the practical aspects of situations like the one they were in. I was moved by the parents' understanding and respect for their daughter's relationship and I was impressed by their recognition that it was only natural for the girl to decide the matters of her partner. After all, they were the ones living together, sharing life's pleasures and pains. But, legally, there was no way she could sign the consent for the surgery. The girl and the parents agreed that the patient should be given a chance with surgery and the father, who had legal authority under the circumstances, signed the consent.

During surgery, after I opened the skull and removed the blood clot. I had to quickly close the dural layer over the brain because I could already see that the brain was beginning to swell and, if I didn't hurry, it could prevent me from being able to close the skull at all. I closed the skull, holding the fractures together with plates and screws, but before I closed the dura, a profound thought crossed my mind as I was looking at the brain. It occurred to me that I could not tell any difference between the brain of a lesbian girl and the brains of straight girls on whom I have operated. They looked the same, pulsated rhythmically with every heartbeat and bruised the same. It's also true when it comes to people of different faiths. I could never tell if I was operating on a Christian, Jewish, Muslim or Hindu brain, and I have operated on all of them. What is this big deal that many people make about the differences among people? I am especially perplexed when people who call themselves religious make distinctions between themselves and people of other faiths or between homosexuals and heterosexuals, so much so that they are hateful and violent towards them? Never made any sense to me.

Unfortunately, over the next two days, the brain swelling was impossible to control and the patient passed away, as I had expected she would. It was impossible to survive such a severe head injury. During those two days the parents stayed in the hospital for most of the time, but her partner never left the hospital. She was at her bedside, holding her hand and crying a lot. I could tell her that she loved her very much. I never felt once that her sorrow was any less than that of a spouse in a heterosexual relationship. Whether they were straight or gay, Christian or Muslim, Hindu or Jewish, I never saw any distinction when it came to how they reacted to personal and family tragedies. They hurt and cried the same in sad situations, and smiled the same on happy occasions. The patients went through the same recovery process no matter what their religious and sexual preferences were. When they were in pain, we gave them the same kind of morphine to alleviate it. There is no straight or gay morphine, or Christian or Jewish or Muslim morphine.

When I meet people, it is never of any concern to me what their religious faiths or sexual lifestyles are. To me there are only good and not so good people. Humanity, fundamentally, is the same no matter which part of the world you come from. All that matters to me is if they are humanistic or not. Sadly, even though the essence of all religions says that we should love others like we want them to love us, differences in beliefs make many people prejudiced, preventing universal brotherhood to prevail.

I believe faith is a double-edged sword. It can do wonders, give solace, comfort, strength and hope for people who need it. On the other hand it can also be a dividing rather than uniting force among people. For that reason, in my view, faith should be confined to what it is meant to be, strictly personal. It is not at all unusual to see that once individual faith spills out of one's personal sphere of life it can lead to friction with other people of different faiths. It can even make people hateful of fellow humans to the extent of killing them. History, as well as contemporary times, is full of conflicts attesting to that fact.

We are only seemingly different in our faiths, beliefs and sexual preferences. I have seen the brains of all different people and know them inside out, and I can promise you that deep down we are all the same. If instead of superficial appearances and different faiths being the dominating influences of our interaction with others, love, compassion, kindness and humanity are the driving emotions behind our relationships with fellow humans, I am confident this world would be a better place. Certainly it will be more peaceful than the troubling times we are living in right now. But unfortunately, the emotion of religious faith dominates and submerges those other emotions.

I may be naïve, but every time I hear John Lennon's song "Imagine," I feel good that I am not the only one feeling that way.

*　　　*　　　*

"When 'I' and 'You' do not exist,
what is mosque? What is synagogue?
What is temple of fire?"

—Sa'd al-din Mahmud Shabstain

> **"Who so neglects learning in his youth, loses the past and is dead for the future."**
>
> —Euripides

Second Chance

Beep, beep, beep, beep, beep.

I woke up from a very deep sleep. It was not a pleasant way to wake up, to the annoying sound of the pager. It was close to midnight. I went to bed just an hour earlier after a long day of surgeries. But I was still on call.

I did not open my eyes, but felt for my beeper on my bedside table and pressed the button that stopped the beeping. I turned on the lamp and looked at the message on the beeper, squinting at the bright light. I was hoping the call wasn't an emergency.

It was.

I called the ER and the secretary connected me to the trauma surgeon.

"Hello, this is Dr. Palavali," I said with a somewhat sleepy voice.

"Hi. Dr. Palavali, I'm sorry to wake you up, but I have a 15 year old kid in the ER, shot in the head;" the trauma surgeon paused very briefly and then continued.

"I think he needs surgery right away, Doc. His right pupil is blown and he is comatose. The head CT scan shows a large blood clot in the right occipital area. There is a 7mm midline shift. We intubated him."

With my attention awakened, I said, "Please give him a gram per kilogram mannitol to keep the pressure down and call the operating room for a craniotomy. Check all his labs and make sure they are OK."

"Yes, Doctor."

"Please have some blood typed and screened and take the patient to the OR. I'll be right there," I said hurriedly.

"Will do, Doc."

"And have the family go up to the waiting room."

"Nobody is here yet but his dad is on the way. I'll send him up."

"Thank you," I said and hung up.

I went into the bathroom, splashed some cold water on my face and quickly got dressed. It was a situation in which a few minutes delay would mean the difference between life and death.

When the trauma surgeon told me that the right pupil was blown, the patient's survival clock started ticking. A blown pupil is an ominous sign suggesting severe pressure on the brain. It meant that the possible consequences were rapid death or prolonged coma if the pressure was not released soon.

Our adrenaline levels go up in high-pressure situations, hence the heightened alertness and anxiety. I sped a little on the way to the hospital. As I pulled into the parking lot, I started to wonder how he got shot. What I heard later was frightening.

Steve's CAT scan showed a big blood clot near the right occipital lobe (the back part of the brain), putting pressure on his brain and pushing it to the left side. When I examined him on the operating table he was comatose. I could see the bullet entry wound in the back of his head. The wound was small and unimpressive and did not reflect the potentially fatal damage caused. His right pupil was dilated and was not reacting to light, which meant that the pressure on the brain was so high that it caused herniation of the brain, a condition in which the brain being pushed caused compression of the third cranial nerve against the brain stem (the part controlling breathing, heart function and consciousness), resulting in coma. If the pressure was not relieved emergently, he might not recover from the coma and could end up brain dead.

After prepping, I got to the brain by making an incision in the scalp and making a window in the skull. The covering of the brain was tense to the touch, due to the underlying pressure. I could see a spot in the dura where the bullet ripped through. The severe pressure was making some of the blood clot and dead brain protrude through that tiny bullet hole. As soon as I made a larger opening in the dura the blood clot spilled out. The bullet, a small piece of twisted and broken metal, came out along with the clot. I removed the blood clot as fast as I could. I stopped the bleeding from the torn blood vessels. The brain started to pulsate in sync with the heartbeat, which meant the pressure in the brain was taken care of. I started to relax a little but, until that time, the sense of hurry and tension in the room was palpable.

After making sure that there was no active bleeding I started to close the dura with a suture. Now that the worst part of the whole situation was past, I wanted to find out how the kid got shot.

"By the way, how did this happen?" I asked our PA.

"You're not gonna believe it, Doc. This kid, his girlfriend and another friend rode a goods train from a small town south of here. They got off at the northern part of town, not a good place to be at night. Looks like they were trying to score some drugs. A few guys from a gang told them to meet at a school there. I don't know exactly what happened but the other guy was shot dead…"

"No," I said in disbelief.

"Yes, Doc. And that's not the end of the story. Then they shot this kid in the head and some of the boys made the girl perform oral sex."

I couldn't believe what I was hearing.

"Afterwards the girl was shot in the face. The gang got out of there. The girl walked to nearby store and got help."

"What happened to her?"

"She's alive. Luckily the bullet only hit her jaw. She is

awake and talking but her face got busted. She's admitted in the pediatric ICU."

"How old is she?"

"Sixteen."

I couldn't stop shaking my head at the story I just heard. I had only read about such terrifying incidents before.

The bone piece was anchored to the rest of the skull with wire. Once the scalp was sutured together and the drapes were removed, I opened his right eye and looked at his pupil. It was normal size. That was a good sign. Hopefully, a life had been saved.

I went to the surgery waiting room and the boy's father was there. I explained everything to him about Steve's condition and what I did. I told him it was too early to tell how he was going to do; though the surgery took care of the immediate problem, he was not out of the woods yet.

He nodded his head as if he understood and thanked me, but what he said after stunned me. "We are going to find the guys who did this to my son. A bunch of my family will come up here and if we have to we'll destroy the entire town."

I was not sure if he truly meant that or if he was just being very emotional and angry. One thing was sure, though. He was drunk.

As I was driving home on the empty and quiet roads into the darkness ahead of me, I reflected on the story of the boy I just operated on. How scary was the devastation that drugs cause on young people's lives! It was a matter of death in Steve's friend's case, permanent disfigurement in the case of his girlfriend and a close call for Steve.

I wondered if most teenagers ever come across those kinds of experiences or similar stories. In spite of situations like Steve's, why would young people still pursue the devastating path of drug addiction and self-destruction?

Everybody knows kids of that age feel invincible. I myself was a teenager once and, although never involved in drugs, I certainly felt there was nothing that could stop me from doing whatever I wanted to do. But I didn't want to do something that would kill me.

I reached home and called the OR to delay the next morning's elective surgeries. I needed some sleep before I could perform anymore surgery.

Over the next few days I was very happy to see that Steve survived his near-death situation. On the second day of surgery, the breathing tube was taken out. On the next day, he was gradually able to sit in a chair and slowly started to walk. A few days later, he walked out of the hospital without any perceivable difference compared to before his ordeal, except the staples that were holding the scalp incision together.

Steve was truly lucky. It was as if he had a second chance on life. I hoped he would realize that and stay away from whatever led him into this trouble.

Next time he might not get a second chance.

I saw Steve and his father a few weeks later in my office for a routine follow-up visit. He was doing well from surgical point of view. I never asked him directly what happened that night. I did not want to stir up horrible memories.

As I was removing the staples, I couldn't believe that I was hearing, for the second time, what Steve's father told me the day I met him after surgery.

"We're gonna come back and destroy the kids that shot Steve and decimate the town, Doc." Steve nodded his head in agreement.

I was shocked to hear what he was saying. The guy must be drunk or high or stupid! I did not know how to respond in that situation but thought to myself these guys were not getting it. Steve almost died. He got a second chance. If I were his father, I would sober up and straighten up.

Should I be lecturing them about the perils of drug addiction? No. It's not that they did not know about the mental, moral, social and financial deterioration addiction causes. After all, they were living it everyday.

A brief lecture by me was probably not going to make any impact. Besides, I was not an addiction counselor. I was just a brain surgeon.

I just told them that from my point of view there was nothing more I needed to do. If there were any questions or if they needed any help, they should call me anytime.

I left the examination room, went into my office and slowly lowered myself into a chair. I was astonished to see that that experience did not influence Steve and his dad to rethink the way they might want to live their lives, away from drugs and violence. I would have thought an ordeal like that would affect anyone. But that was not the case. Steve may have thought he was invincible, but he doesn't realize how close he came to dying.

I was not sure if Steve was the way he was because he was young and did not know better or because his father had such a bad influence on him. I was not sure if I should be angry with Steve or pity him.

At that moment I decided to write his story. I hoped that,

if he were not going to learn from this tragedy, at least somebody else could, because not everybody gets a second chance.

*   *   *

**"I expect to pass through life but once.
If, therefore, there be any kindness I can show
or any good thing I can do to any fellow
being, let me do it now, for I shall not
pass this way again."**

—William Penn

"Since non-existence (Death) is our own inescapable destiny we should make the best of the only life we have. The good life in this life, happiness in this world, should be our aim. And because both our physical health and the maintenance of good personal relationships require it, we should enjoy our pleasures in moderation, though no non-injurious activity needs to be regarded as forbidden in itself."

—Epicurus

The Middle Path

I wonder about it a lot. Life!

That is, what it is all about, the meaning of it and the best way to live it. I suppose there is no single right way of living, and the meaning of life, I believe, is what one makes it out to be.

Some live for today, highly hedonistic. Others live for an unknown afterlife, ascetically depriving themselves of even simple worldly pleasures. And there is a whole range of options in between. Fortunately, that gives us a lot of latitude for ways of living life and allows interesting diversity.

I think that's very good; it makes life exciting.

I do have a problem about addiction. Addiction is physical, mental and moral deterioration and it is not healthy for the body or mind. Things that are so detrimental, even in little doses, are not good in life. Steve and his friends' tragic story is but one example of many that occur daily in the world. I am not sure what makes people become addicted. Is it the pursuit of hedonism or the lack of discipline to live a proportionate life? It is probably a complex problem involving genetics, environmental influences and temptation, and one's ability to discipline oneself so as not to succumb to it.

Furthermore, as pleasurable as it may seem, unrestrained hedonism, even if it is not bordering on addiction, is not good either. Even the finest of epicurean delights will not taste as delicious in excess as they do in the beginning. I think a little bit of deprivation keeps us longing for more. (All the married men know that truth. Throughout time, wives have figured that out and I am convinced that is the reason for depriving their husbands of much-desired sex.)

The middle path is the way when it comes to enjoying most of the hedonistic pleasures in life. But when it comes to drugs, "just saying no" is the best way, as I am reminded every time I see a patient with a broken blood vessel in the brain causing a huge blood clot, which is seen, not uncommonly, in people using cocaine.

I myself like Epicurus' advice. It is amazing that he correctly figured out, centuries ago, that the body is made of atoms and, when they are associated in complementary fashion and working properly, there is life; and when they are disrupted or disassociated, there is death. Simple and brilliant! Nothing about soul, heaven and afterlife. Additionally, he said to emphasize one's only life in this world and to live it fully. In fact his views and understanding were so radical they might have been misunderstood to be blasphemous and put his and his followers' lives in danger for heresy. He had a solution for that. People of like- mindedness should get together and enjoy their lives quietly. Unfortunately he was misunderstood as preaching extreme hedonism. He was not; he preached moderation.

A simple anecdote that my father told me, when I was young, comes to mind. Winston Churchill was once asked to say in one word what he thought was the most important thing to keep in mind in one's life. He thought about it for a moment and said, "Proportion." Now that I am older I truly recognize the wisdom of that anecdote. Proportion: sounds like balance and moderation to me. The "middle path," as Buddha called it.

It is difficult to follow the middle path. (Even though Buddha preached it, he led an ascetic life. I don't understand why!) Unrestrained hedonism (as tempting as it sounds) will not keep one happy forever. Besides, the brain develops tolerance to even the best of pleasures. On the other hand, living a self-imposed monastic and deprived way in your one and only lifetime is a waste of precious life, in my view. So I chose to take the middle path.

It took me a long time, many years, before I could realize that.

We don't have to have the most expensive material things or lead a complex, multi- tasking life, working like mad. Even if one takes away life's fleshy (and flashy) layers of pretences, self-created complexities, self-imposed inhibitions, confusion, delusions and misconceptions, one can still find life enchanting in its simplest form. In fact, the minimal way of life may be even more rewarding than it's opposite. I think many of us are looking for and trying to achieve such an easy, simple and balanced life, but it has not proven easy to attain.

Even though I agree with Buddha's advice about the "middle path," I disagree with his conclusion that life is all suffering. Life is day and night, pleasure and pain, joy and sadness, hard work and laziness, emotions soaring as high as tall mountains and sinking as deep as dark abyss, punishment and reward, elation and misery and, simply, life itself and death. It can be a balance of all these and frankly any of these extremes is not good for one's body or mind. It is possible that I am fortunate enough to be in a social and financial condition that allows me to feel that way. I don't know if I would have a positive or hopeful attitude if I were being crushed by the burden of poverty or loneliness. I know there are millions of people much less fortunate than I am, but I am hopeful that those lives can be altered by the collective humane efforts of the fortunate among us, thus helping them feel that life is a joyous experience. A centered life, I believe, is the right way to live.

*   *   *

"It is wealth to be content."

—Lao-Tzu

> "Holidays are more than meals. They are celebrations of togetherness."
>
> —Unknown

Merry Christmas

I was stunned. I was looking at the brain MRI as the pictures came up on the monitor. I had a suspicion that I would find something abnormal, but did not expect to see the huge tumor that I was staring at. For a minute my heart sank into my stomach and started beating faster. The tumor was on the left side, where the speech center is, and was so big that it was pushing the brain to the opposite side. That explains the headaches she was complaining about for a few weeks. Also, the part of the brain that deals with the memory was being compressed. No wonder she could not remember where she left her car keys and where she parked her car. After I recovered from the initial shock of that unexpected finding on the MRI, I started thinking like a brain surgeon. I could tell that the tumor was under the covering of the brain and outside, rather than inside, the brain. Those tumors are called meningiomas and are usually benign. Also they can be removed completely through surgery most of the time. My heart settled down a little bit but I still was very anxious and looked at the patient lying down in the MRI tunnel. The patient was my wife.

The whole thing started the evening before while I was packing to go to a weekend conference in Pittsburgh. My flight was around 11 in the morning. My wife came to me and said, just as a matter of fact, "Vivek, I was driving this morning with Surya (my 4 year old son) sleeping in the back seat. Suddenly my right leg became numb and I could not move it for a couple of minutes. I had to pull over to the side of the road and stop the car. Fortunately I was on a small road that was not busy. After a couple minutes I was able to feel my leg and move it." I stopped what I was doing and looked at her.

I could not believe what she had said. "What? That sounds like a seizure to me. How come you didn't call me right away? You shouldn't have continued to drive. You could have had another seizure and ended up in an accident. You were lucky. I can't believe you didn't call me!" I repeated in dismay. "You should get an MRI of your brain tomorrow morning." I don't think I could control the anxiety in my voice.

She said she was not going to have an MRI done until I came back from the trip and even then she was going to think about it. I told her that she was not comprehending the seriousness of what I was suggesting and she should get the MRI done the next morning. In fact, for the past few weeks she was taking more headache medicine than usual and I told her a few times to get a CAT scan of her brain to see if there were any problems. As a brain surgeon, I can make my patients listen to my advice, but not my wife. But this time I knew there could be something terribly wrong. She still would not listen to me and said that there was no way she was going to have the test done the next day. This time I was not going to listen to her! I picked up the phone and called the MRI tech and scheduled the test for 8 a.m. the next day. If the MRI did not show any abnormality, I was going to have one of my neurologist colleagues see her to determine if she needed any medication, if he thought she had a seizure. Of course, I was hoping that the MRI would be negative for any abnormalities. That didn't end up being the case.

I have seen a lot of tumors similar to this in my practice. This one was different. It was in my wife's head. I have explained to the patients and their families about these tumors and that they may need surgery many times in the past but, at that moment, as my wife got up and walked out of that MRI room, I was groping for words about how to tell her that she has a large tumor pressing on her brain. She had one of those hospital gowns on. Since I didn't know how to break the bad news, I thought I would start with something that would lessen the shock to follow. I told her that she looked cute in that hospital gown and that she should add it to her wardrobe. I knew it was silly but I didn't know how else to start the conversation. I thought I might as well say it right away, as we walked out of the MRI room.

I put my hand on her shoulders and told her, "Honey, I have some bad news and some good news for you. Let me start with the bad news first. The bad news is that you have a tumor in your head. The good news is that it looks like a benign tumor and we should be able to get rid of this with surgery. I do not wish anybody to have a tumor but if somebody has one, this is the one to have."

She looked at me with an expression of trying to figure out if I was serious or joking. I told her I was serious and took her to the MRI viewing board where her brain scans were hanging. I showed her the tumor and assured her that we would take care of it as soon as possible. I didn't think she really understood the gravity of the situation.

I immediately called one of my neurologist colleagues and he put her on anti-seizure medication. Next, I called one of the surgeons who I know well and told him about my wife. He told me to bring her that evening and he could see her after his surgeries. Needless to say I canceled my trip and drove her and my four year old son home. As I was driving, many different thoughts stirred in my mind. I have always been on the doctor's side of the fence but never on the side of the family of a patient. This was an unexpected and unbelievably scary experience. I thought of how our lives would be changed if something went wrong with my wife and how that would devastate me and my boys, who are still very young. I tried to shut out those thoughts and stay positive. It was just a week before Christmas. The day after Christmas we had airline tickets booked to go to India to see my family. As we were waiting for the evening to consult the surgeon, I called my travel agent and canceled the trip. I called my mother- and sister-in-law and told them about my wife. We immediately arranged to have my mother-in-law fly in from Washington, D.C. that night. After consulting the neurosurgeon, we were going to pick her up from the airport. It probably was not going to be a joyful Christmas.

That evening the surgeon saw my wife. He repeated the same things that I told her before we met him. There was no question that she needed surgery. The question was when. My wife wanted to wait until after Christmas to have it done. As a neurosurgeon looking at the extent of pressure the tumor was putting on her brain, I wanted the surgery done as soon as possible. My wife insisted on waiting but I told her that taking care of this problem was more important and we could celebrate Christmas any time. She wanted to think about it. Later that night we picked up my mother-in-law and, over the next day, we discussed the surgery. Finally I convinced my wife to have it as soon as she could. She needed some additional tests, called cerebral angiograms, the day before surgery to evaluate the blood supply to the tumor and to block the arteries going to the tumor (embolisation) in order to decrease the possibility of excessive bleeding during surgery. The surgery was set for two days before Christmas.

Those next four days prior to surgery were the worst days I experienced. My wife was unbelievably stoic and poised and held herself together. I could not believe how strong and courageous she was. Some friends came to know about this situation and visited us. They couldn't believe how well my wife was handling it. As a neurosurgeon, my biggest concern was that, if there were any bleeding in the tumor while we were waiting for the surgery, my wife could either die or have a severe stroke. There was also a very good possibility that she could not speak because of the location of the tumor. Those were the worst thoughts that I had to deal with every moment until her surgery. I tried my best to distract myself and push them to the back of my mind. But I had to have a plan in case she did have bleeding, which would require emergent surgery. The hospital where she was going to have surgery was more than an hour and a half away. I knew that would be too long to wait in case of emergency. Any bleeding in the tumor would push the already compressed brain more and make her comatose. I would have to call the paramedics to immediately put a tube into her lungs to breathe; I would also have to call the OR of the hospital where I do most of my surgeries, which is half an hour away, to be on standby and, as soon as a head CAT scan was performed to see how bad the bleeding was, I might have to do the surgery myself if my partner were not available. That was a hard thought to deal with. I couldn't imagine the idea of opening my wife's skull and operating on her brain. If anything went wrong during surgery, I wonder if I would be able to complete it. For the first time I could clearly experience all the thoughts, fears, worries and anxieties that families go through before their loved ones undergo surgery. I had some idea about it but, now that I lived through it, I could fully sympathize with them. I had all the unpleasant and terrifying thoughts of how, if she became comatose, our young boys would be deprived of the love, comfort and care that only a mother can give and I, of the companionship of my life partner. It would be almost impossible to deal with. I have tremendous respect for all the people who are in those situations and are managing their lives, still able to bring a smile to their faces.

The day before surgery, my-mother-in law and I took my

wife to the hospital. She had an angiogram and the arteries going to the tumor could be blocked successfully; she was taken to the ICU for observation because the tumor could swell and put more pressure on the brain, requiring immediate surgery. I rented an apartment on the hospital campus. That night, my wife's brother and sister visited her and brought my two boys from home. My little boy was overwhelmed by the intensive care unit and wanted to get out of that place as soon as possible. I left my wife around 11 p.m. to enable her to get some rest. I had a restless sleep that night and couldn't wait for the morning for surgery to be started. I set the alarm to wake me up at 6 a.m. because the surgery was set for 8 o'clock. The radio woke me up to one of my favorite jazz songs. I sat up in bed listening to the song, trying to control my anxiety and anticipation. Then, one of my all-time favorite songs, "What a Wonderful World" by Louis Armstrong, came on the radio. That song hit something deep within me and tears ran down my cheeks. I felt that the wonderful life that I have right now with my wife could end if something happened to her during surgery.

I got up, got ready quickly and went to the hospital an hour before her scheduled surgery time. I felt very sad when I saw my wife in the ICU. She must've cried during the night. Her eyes were red and her eyelids were puffy. That was the first time I saw her, during the entire time we were waiting for surgery, that she looked scared and shaken. The weather during the day seemed to have the same mood. There was a heavy snow storm and it snowed relentlessly. For a while we were concerned if the surgeon was going to make it to the hospital or not. Fortunately he was able to, but my wife's brother and sister got slowed down by the storm and could not make it on time. Luckily, she was able to talk to them on phone, barely a few minutes before she was taken into the operating room. As they started wheeling her away, I told her that I loved her and gave her a kiss. She said she loved me, too. For a second, I had the unbearable thought that there was a possibility that this might be the last time she could ever tell me that she loved me.

During the surgery, my mother-in-law and I were in the surgery waiting room and, after awhile, my brother- and sister-in-law joined us. As I was waiting, my mind was automatically going step-by-step through the surgery that was taking place a few rooms away. I was hoping that no injury would occur to her brain. Usually I am in the OR performing the surgery and not the one pacing the floor of the waiting room. This time it was my turn to sit and anxiously wait for the surgeon to come and say that everything went fine. I could personally live through and understand, moment by moment, what the patients' families go through as I am operating on their loved ones. It was a unique experience, but I hope it was the last one of its kind. My partner was caring enough to drive from miles away in that snowy weather to periodically peek in the OR and come back to inform me that everything was going well. For three hours that felt like eternity, we waited until the surgeon came and told us the good news.

The neurosurgeon side of me had to see her to check and make sure, with my own eyes, that she was talking and moving her arms and legs before I could settle down. As I was conducting my "neuro-assessment" of her, she told me not to bother her and to leave her alone. My wife was back to herself! I was never happier to be bossed by her.

Over the next few days, during the recovery process, she

had to endure some headaches and some memory problems before they eventually cleared out. Three days after surgery I brought her home. We celebrated, belatedly, the most meaningful and truly happiest Christmas. The joy of knowing that everything was fine with my wife could not be expressed in words, as everybody gathered around the Christmas tree. One by one we opened our gifts. All seven kids (nephew, nieces and our boys) were smiling, laughing and happy about their presents. But that evening, all of us had an unsaid understanding that the most precious gift of all was my wife's well-being. That day, the universal and eternal truth that love, health and family togetherness are the most important things that anybody could wish for was deeply felt by everybody around that beautiful and glittering tree.

All the life lessons that I learned from the hard and painful experiences of my patients and their families had already shaped my philosophy to live, love and enjoy life as fully as possible everyday. The personal experience of living through my wife's ordeal summed up all those experiences and strengthened my resolve to practice that philosophy. It enhanced my ability to appreciate the joy of this journey called life, which I intend to relish deeply and exquisitely, with my loved ones, until I die.

*　　　*　　　*

"Mid pleasures and palaces we may roam, be it ever so humble, there's no place like home."

—J.H. Payne

"Life is a journey, not a destination."

—Unknown

Enjoy the Journey

It was a perfectly round and red sun rising in the horizon over a silvery sheet of the calm waters of Lake Michigan. It was 6 a.m. I was driving on Lake Shore Drive in Chicago towards Hyde Park on the way to the University of Chicago Hospital. I was a second-year resident in neurosurgery at that time.

I was driving slowly as I had more time than usual before starting the morning rounds in the intensive care unit at 6:30

a.m. I did not feel rushed as I would have most days and was enjoying the scenery outside the car window.

That's when I saw that spectacular sunrise.

It was a June morning. I had the window of the car rolled down and could feel the cool, fresh wind hitting my face. It was a perfect moment, a moment in which I felt as one with nature. (Being a very busy neurosurgical resident, I didn't have many of those moments. All the more reason to cherish it!)

The beauty of the sunrise reflecting over the still waters was mesmerizing. I almost felt like stopping the car and going to the water's edge to enjoy the morning without worrying about going to work. (Needless to say, I could not do so. As a resident, you better have a damn good reason not to go to the hospital.) It felt like a special morning.

But, wait a minute...it was not a special day. That sunrise was not unlike most others on June mornings. How come I did not give much attention to sunrises past? I had been driving on Lake Shore Drive for more than two years. I hardly recall many such mornings. What was different that particular day?

As I thought about that, it occurred to me that it was not the sunrise that was different; instead it was one of the rare mornings where I did not feel rushed on the way to work. Most of the time during my residency, the days were so busy and hectic that I used to feel hard-pressed for time and was living a hurried life. In the process I was oblivious to the beauty that surrounded me. Even though my body was in the present, my mind was a step ahead into the future, already thinking about all the things I had to do that day and my plans for dealing with them. In that way, not only I was missing out the present, I was getting stressed about a future that had not arrived yet.

I was not taking one moment at a time. Even when my body was walking, I was mostly running in my mind. The body and mind were not in step. I must have not been living the way Buddha wanted people to live, in the present moment.

That simple yet deep realization that day has been helping my mind since then to get grounded in the present rather than taking unnecessary and anxiety-provoking flights into the future. I learned to come to my senses and get control of my thoughts in times of hurried and stressful situations, mostly created by myself, in my mind.

In addition it helped me slow down and clear my mind so that the beauty of the world and life around me could wash over me. I did not have to specifically look for beautiful things around me. All I had to do was stay in the present moment and allow my senses to be stimulated the way they were naturally supposed to. My constantly preoccupied and cluttered mind was clouding my senses from perceiving the surrounding pleasure and beauty that was everywhere.

Each and every one of my senses could be stimulated pleasantly and effortlessly. Let me count the ways, for example, that June morning:

- The beautiful sunrise pleasing my eyes,
- The sounds of birds chirping like nature's music,
- The cool and fresh wind caressing the skin on my face,

- The lilacs' fragrance making me take a deep breath,

As I said, I felt one with nature.

For that short but sweet period I felt alive, careless, worriless, weightless and happy.

Yes! Pure happiness.

As I said, it felt like a perfect moment. I wanted that moment to stay frozen in time for a while. I believed life was full of those moments, if only we slowed down in our minds and let life happen to all our senses.

Since that day I gradually learned to take moment by moment, hour by hour and day by day, one at a time. It took me time and frequent reminders to myself to concentrate on the present, thus making me live in the present as much as possible and prevent my mind from racing into the future.

You cannot do what you want to do or enjoy what you are doing unless you detach your mind from the wheels of a sense of urgency churning in your head. This is not a small matter. It means having a happy life, an enjoyable career or a restful and relaxing vacation.

I had a friend during first-year residency who was looking forward so much to going home at the end of each call day that any delay in leaving due to unexpected patient problems that needed to be taken care of were making her very upset. She told me that it was so upsetting to her that she was beginning to hate her patients. She quit being a surgery resident and became an ER resident because of the more predictable hours. But she loved being a surgery resident. If she could have accepted the fact that she was going to have some unexpected events due to the nature of her residency training and took one problem at a time and dealt with them, instead of constantly thinking about the next hour, she might have been less stressed. She probably could have continued in training to become a surgeon. That was her first love and what she always wanted to be. Now she has to settle for her second choice.

I always remembered her state of mind and usually avoid getting into that sense of disharmony among the body, mind and time. Yes, one should have a plan, organization and direction for everyday, but there is no point in thinking about the evening already even before you start your day in the morning. There is no sense in thinking of getting out of there even before you get there.

In my constantly busy and pressed-for-time way of life, that mantra of living in the moment and dealing with things as they come keeps me sane and suits me just fine. It usually allows me to smile as much as I can under the circumstances. It makes me enjoy being in the operating room, interacting with my colleagues and patients and coming home to my beautiful family with a smile, most days. That, in turn, makes people enjoy being with me, I think.

Rushing in your mind prevents you from experiencing the current moment and life to its fullest depth, with vigor. Having your mind somewhere else and in the distant future rather than here and now prevents you from being either in the present or the future, for it is impossible to be in both at the same time. The only possible way to be and live is to be and live in the present moment. Many a Zen master said time and again to completely immerse ourselves and be acutely aware of the present moment.

Somebody once said while you were thinking about the future, it just came and went.

No doubt there is pleasure and a sense of accomplishment in reaching the goal or destination. On the other hand the journey itself could be pleasurable and wondrous. We are usually so engrossed with the idea of reaching our goals or destination that it occupies and clouds the mind so much, distracting us from the present as it passes by us one second at a time. Only an undistracted and free mind will have a chance to really grasp the surrounding beauty of life along the journey.

Another important truth that I learned is that, by erasing preconceived notions, misconceptions and delusions and making my mind as clean a slate as possible, devoid of clutter, the beauty of life etches itself into my mind unfiltered and with immediacy.

This principle of enjoying the journey without being engrossed too much by the destination is applicable not only to day-to-day life, but also to the very essence of living a full and enjoyable lifetime.

So take it easy, relax and enjoy the journey. You will reach the destination when you do and, at that time, you will have all the time to enjoy where you are, a sense of accomplishment and the pleasure of reaching your goal.

*   *   *

"As you walk and eat and travel, be where you are. Otherwise you will miss most of your life."

—The Buddha

"To the mind that is still the whole
universe surrenders."

—Lao-Tzu

"We think in eternity, but we move
slowly through time."

—Oscar Wilde

"The only way to live life is through the
consumption of the present moment. Life
happens with successive "now" moments."

—Arthur Schopenhauer

"Those in a hurry do not arrive."

—Zen saying

> '**Remember this—that very little is needed to make a happy life.**"
>
> —Marcus Aurelius

Chocolate

I just finished a 4-hour long surgery. The patient was young. She was just 35 years old.

I removed a tumor from the front part of her brain on the left side. It was a malignant metastatic tumor.

I walked into the postoperative recovery room and sat down. Usually it felt good to sit down after a long, successful surgery, but not that day. Even though the surgery went without any problems, the thought of brain cancer in a young patient always made me feel defeated. Every time I come across a situation like that, no matter how long I might have been in practice, I always felt sad because a young and enthusiastic life would come to an end too soon.

I was quietly writing the postoperative orders when I heard, "Hi, Dr. Palavali."

I looked up and saw Michelle, the hospital's surgical liaison. She would be the one to keep the families of patients who were being operated on comfortable and inform them when the surgery started, if everything was going alright and when the surgery was done.

She must have noticed the expression on my face. She knew right away that the long-term prognosis of the patient was not good.

"You don't have good news for the family, do you, Doctor?" Michelle asked.

I responded simply by nodding my head.

She became quiet for a minute or so and asked, "She's young, isn't she?"

I nodded in agreement, again.

Michelle was a very nice person, caring, pleasant and good with people. I always enjoyed seeing her in the hospital and, in fact, would strike up conversations with her often. Sometimes those would be philosophical and profound since, being a doctor, I came across situations that made me reflect on the fragility of life. I could not help but express to Michelle what was going on in my mind at that moment.

"Michelle, this is why I tell everybody to enjoy life everyday as much as possible. You never know what bad stuff is going to hit you and when."

"I know exactly what you mean, Doctor. In fact a close friend of mine died recently from breast cancer. She was very young, too."

I shook my head but examples like that were not new or surprising to me. In my line of work coming across such situations was not infrequent.

I continued reiterating my point. "I keep telling everybody not to put off enjoying life. Life is too short."

"I know," Michelle echoed the sentiment and said something that strongly impressed me.

"Doc, I remember one day my friend told me that before she was diagnosed with cancer, she was watching her diet very strictly and did not eat any chocolate even though she loved it very much. But when she was diagnosed with cancer and was dying she wondered why she didn't eat chocolate whenever she felt like eating it. It made no sense to her, in the big scheme of life, that she deprived herself of life's simple pleasures and suddenly she was going to die and nothing really mattered. It was too late to do all the little things that she always wanted to do but did not think were important or worth thinking about. She could not understand, in a philosophical sense, why people did not live their daily lives with the perspective that it could all end suddenly so they should let themselves live a little. Now that she was facing imminent death, all those little things that didn't seem to matter before suddenly seemed to be what life was all about. Now, even if she ate all the chocolate she could, it really didn't matter because she was going to die soon. Doc, my heart broke when she told me that."

Michelle paused for a moment and then resumed. "I agree with you, Doc. We postpone lots of things for the future. We don't have our priorities right. I will never forget what my friend said. We have to put our whole life in perspective and take one day at a time and get the best out of that day. No matter how simple of a thing it may be, like eating chocolate, you have to do it today. You may not get another chance or your life may take an unexpected turn."

"I couldn't agree with you more, Michelle."

From that day onwards I never forgot Michelle's friend's words. I could completely understand what her friend must have gone through. In the course of a day, I come across many patients suffering from many different afflictions of the brain, spinal cord and nerves. These patients end up not being able to do simple things and enjoy simple pleasures that would usually be taken for granted by millions of people. During my practice, I saw patients with breathing tubes in their mouths begging for a sip of water; stroke patients with tubes in their stomachs to prevent them from choking when they tried to swallow, longing for a bite of a burger; patients with paralyzed legs saying they would do anything to be able to walk just one step; patients in chronic pain saying they would love to have one good night of sleep; patients dying with brain tumors regretting not taking the vacation they always wished to take; and families of patients in comas sitting next to the bed, waiting eagerly for them to just open their eyes and look at them just once more.

None of these are extraordinary feats and, in fact, are so routine that we take them for granted, until we get into an unfortunate situation when we cannot do them anymore. Then we long for life's ordinary and simple pleasures.

Why, then, do we wait to realize this until some devastation occurs in our lives? Why don't we enjoy a glass of water, a slow walk, a good meal, a good night's sleep and our loved ones, each and every day? Why don't we take a little vacation when we feel the desire? I am not saying that we should be unrealistic and overdo beyond our means. All I am saying is to enjoy and relish life within our means while we can. The story about Michelle's friend and her love of chocolate represents to me that simple yet profound philosophy of how we should live life.

I am just happy to realize that aspect about living without having gone through any personal tragedy, like Michelle's friend did. But I will never forget her words about chocolate. In fact, if you'll excuse me, I want to go and have some right now.

*   *   *

"Exactness in little things is a wonderful source of cheerfulness."

—Frederick William Faber

> "A multitude of simple delights
> constitutes happiness."

> —Anonymous

Let Me Count the Ways

Quietness of early morning

Stillness of dawn

Favorite wake-up music

A few minutes of extra sleep after the alarm goes off

Laying in bed relishing a sweet dream

Just laying in bed without thinking of anything in particular

Changing colors of a morning sky

Red sun, rising over the horizon

Peaceful, sleeping faces of your spouse and kids

Giving them a gentle kiss on their soft cheeks and seeing them smile in their sleep

Stepping outdoors and feeling the fresh, cool, crisp air on your face

Aroma of coffee

Birds chirping

Sunrays filtering through the leaves

Flowers

A butterfly fluttering by

Hummingbirds

Feeling the cold dew drops on the grass with your bare feet

Dew drops on a spider web

Still waters on a misty morning

Fog

Pleasantly painful stretch of muscles while exercising

Coolness of sweat on your tired body

Invigorating sensation of cold water on your face

Warm shower soothing the body

Hot breakfast

Juicy fruit

Woods and fields passing by on the way to work (if you are not working in a city)

Wishing "Good morning" to a colleague at work

Good morning greeting from a colleague

A job well done

Expressing thanks to someone who helped you

Good feeling when somebody thanks you for your kindness

Phone call from a friend after a long time

Sharing a joke with your workmates

Getting a pat on your back for your creativity

Relishing a sandwich when really hungry

Feeling the coolness of a cold drink in your throat on a hot day

Stepping into the outside world at the end of a work day

Just stopping for a minute and recognizing that you are healthy (if you are)

Hot cup of coffee

Beach

Shimmering sea on a mid-summer day

Shells on the beach

Colorful tropical fish

Snorkeling

Palm trees

Clear blue sky

Cumulonimbus clouds

Getting drenched in monsoon rain

Rainbow

Soft velvety moss on a damp rock under a shady tree

Mushrooms on a fallen tree trunk

Waterfall

Feeling the waterfall spray on your face

Ferns

Child running to you with a smile as soon as you enter your house

The "Welcome home" kiss from your loved one

Playing tag with your child

Sitting in the swing along with your kids and listening to crickets (or frogs, depending on where you live)

Watching a blue sky turn yellow then red then pink then purple

Perfectly round red sun disappearing beyond the horizon

Family dinner (in spite of the mess made by the kids)

Stand-up comedy

Starry night

Full moon through the trees

Fireflies

Reading a bedtime story to your child

Reading your favorite book

Just laying down in bed after a long day

Wishing your little one, "'Nighty night, don't let the bed bugs bite"

Giving a hug to your loved one

Saying, "I love you" to your loved one

Hearing your loved one say, "I love you"

Sex (any time the mood strikes)

Dozing off to soft, soothing music

Sweet dream

These constitute just the tip of the iceberg of things and acts that are joyful and priceless, yet do not cost you a thing. Everybody has a list of things that makes them happy or relaxed or serene.

The list could be very long or almost endless, if one can simply be receptive to the joy and beauty in this world.

*   *   *

"Life is a paradise for those who love many things with a passion."

—Leo Buscaglia

"Happiness is a choice, and **you** are the one who's responsible for it."

—Unknown

"May you **live** all the days of **your life**."

—Jonathan Swift

"And, if not **now**, when?"

—Talmud